Daniel Alexander Payne

The Venerable Preceptor of the African Methodist Episcopal Church

Nelson T. Strobert

God's peace to you!

Nelson T. Strobert

UNIVERSITY PRESS OF AMERICA, ® INC.
Lanham • Boulder • New York • Toronto • Plymouth, UK

Copyright © 2012 by
University Press of America,® Inc.
4501 Forbes Boulevard
Suite 200
Lanham, Maryland 20706
UPA Acquisitions Department (301) 459-3366

10 Thornbury Road
Plymouth PL6 7PP
United Kingdom

Library of Congress Control Number: 2012932243
ISBN: 978-0-7618-5867-6 (paperback : alk. paper)
eISBN: 978-0-7618-5868-3

In memory of Eugene Strobert (1926–1994)
and
Earnestine Walker Strobert (1926–2004),
my parents.

Contents

Preface

This book emerged from several encounters I have had with the life story of Daniel Alexander Payne over several decades. I was introduced to Payne while I was pursuing my Master of Divinity degree at Gettysburg Seminary in the early 1970s. During my year at the Lutheran House of Studies in Washington, DC, I took a course at Howard University Divinity School entitled, "History of the Black Church" with Dr. Henry Ferry. In one lecture he mentioned the name Daniel A. Payne who had studied at Gettysburg Lutheran Seminary in Pennsylvania. Although I was a second-year Gettysburg seminarian, that lecture was the first time I had ever heard the name mentioned. From hearing a few short lecture notes on the man, I decided to write my term paper on this formidable figure in the Black Church history.

My second encounter occurred in 1992 when I presented a paper at the International Colloquium—Les Noirs Américains et L'Europe [African Americans in Europe] sponsored by the Du Bois Institute (Harvard University), Centre d'Etudes Afro-américains (Sorbonne Nouvelle) Paris, Center for the Study of Southern Culture (University of Mississippi), and Center for American Cultural Studies (Columbia University). The paper entitled "The Influence of France on the Thought of Daniel Alexander Payne" highlighted his travels in Europe and suggested the manner in which his travels helped to change the curriculum at Wilberforce University.

At the annual meeting of the Association for the Study of African American Life and History in 1995, I presented the paper "Daniel Alexander Payne, Paris and the Cultivation of the African American Educator" where I focused on Payne and his self-education that incorporated Europe.

My curiosity with Payne and his Europe connections continued with a paper I presented in 1997 entitled "Land of the Free and Home of the Brave: The Role of Europe in the Work and Education of Daniel Alexander Payne" at the bi-annual meeting of the Colloquium for African American Research in Muenster, Germany. This paper was later published in *Critical Voices in Black Liberation*. The focus of the presentation was on the sense of freedom that Payne experienced while in Europe which was not his experience in his own native land.

These professional meetings, as well as presentations in seminary class-rooms and conferences, adult forums in churches, and published articles on Payne, helped to bring this book to fruition. I see this study as a biographical portrait of Payne which spans his eighty-two years of life. Through a chrono-logical and thematic framework, I hope the reader gets a picture of the impor-tance of education in African American families and church life regardless of denomination. As Payne helped to shape the lives and minds of students and congregational members in the nineteenth century, I hope the following pages assist us in the twenty-first century to be inspired by Payne's story.

This could not have taken place without assistance from the following institutions which were helpful during the research process: Wilberforce University Library Archives and Ms. Jacqueline Brown, L'Eglise Evangelique Luthérienne—Paris Archives and Pr. Joly, Société d'Histoire de l'Eglise Protestante de France—Paris, TheAmerican Church of Paris Archives, the Archives of the Lutheran Theological Seminary at Gettysburg and Dr. Bohleke, Ms. Roberta Brent and Ms. Susan Posey, Union Theological Seminary in New York Library, The Library of Congress, Bibliothèque Nationale de France, Gettysburg College Special Collections, Adams County Historical Society, Musée National de l'Education—Rouen, France, the Moorland-Spingarn Research Center—Howard University, and the Schomburg Center for Research in Black Culture-New York Public Library.

I must give a personal note of thanks to my present and former colleagues as well as the Board of Directors at the Lutheran Theological Seminary at Gettysburg who granted me sabbatical time to travel, research, and write this volume. A grant from the Association of Theological Schools helped me to engage in the initial research for this book. I give a particular note of thanks to Dr. Barbara J. Ballard who read portions of the text and Dr. Timothy Wal-tonen who gave invaluable time to edit, critique, and encourage me during the final phase of writing.

A special thanks goes to members of the Strobert family who continue to encourage, prod, and support my adventures; especially my sister, Dr. Jeanie Strobert Payne.

Acknowledgments

The photograph of Daniel Alexander Payne is courtesy of the Ohio Historical Society.

The correspondence of Daniel A. Payne to Simon S. Schmucker is courtesy of the Lutheran Theological Seminary, A.R. Wentz Library Seminary Archives, S.S. Schmucker Collection.

Chapter One

The Formative Years: 1811–1837

Daniel A. Payne was born to Martha and London Payne, free persons of color in Charleston, South Carolina on February 24, 1811. Payne recounted his earliest memories of his family life in his autobiography *Recollections of Seventy Years*.[1] These memories of family became a fundamental component for him in later years. Payne recalled that his father would sing hymns and pray aloud which often awakened Daniel early in the morning. In addition to religious nurture, Payne also recalled that London taught him the alphabet and simple spelling words.[2] This fusion of family, church, and learning undergirded Payne's love for the world of education and initiated his interest in theology. London Payne died when Daniel was five years old. Payne suggests that his mother carried on the tradition his father had started; Daniel accompanied her and sat with her on her the class-meetings at church.[3] His mother died a few years later, but those "strong religious feelings" which were developed with his parents continued to grow through the efforts of his aunt Mrs. Sarah Bordeaux.[4] He speaks fondly of her and attributed her with modeling the religious life for him.

STUDENT AND TEACHER

Although Payne's early education was informal, through the family, he eventually was enrolled in the Minor's Moralist School in Charleston. A school owned and operated by free men of color since its founding in 1803. It was designed to provide educational opportunity for orphaned and indigent children. The rules of the organization stated:

> Deceased members who have regularly paid up their contributions to the time of their death, and leaving children, being free heirs in law, in low and indigent

1

circumstances, so that they cannot, out of their estate, be accommodated with learning, in this case, the Society shall, at their expense, teach or cause to be taught, all such children, reading, writing and arithmetic, and also be supported with every necessary of life until arrived at the age of fourteen years, after which they shall be bound out to some good trade, the male to serve until twenty-one years...[5]

Payne was a student there for two years, between eight and ten years of age. These elementary school years, although brief in time, were memorable to our future educator and clergyman. He commented on learning the basic areas of elementary schooling: reading, writing, spelling and arithmetic. While Payne mentioned that he and his fellow students read monographs on the history of Greece, Rome, and England, he identified by name the *Columbian Orator* which was a popular text at the time.[6] His remembering of that particular text is significant for several reasons. The text was one of the most popular in schools during the first half of the nineteenth century. The primary purpose of this book of oratory was "[to] cultivate its rudiments, and diffuse its spirit among the youth of America..."[7] It had significance for the students who attended the school in that this text contained themes that were religious and moralistic.[8] In addition, Bingham was judicious in using texts which were strongly anti-slavery. Students learning to speak and memorize bits and pieces from literature came across such titles as: "The Dignity of Human Nature" by Burges, "Dialogue between a Master and Slave," Dialogue between a White Man and an Indian" by David Everett, "Oration on the Manumission of Slaves" by Miller. These titles indicated the anti-slavery and anti-Southern sentiments of the compiler to the point that Southerners began to advocate speech texts written from Southern perspectives.[9] In a sense the *Columbian Orator* was a textbook of liberation, and it influenced the thinking of the prominent and renowned nineteenth century abolitionist and orator, Frederick Douglass.

Upon completing his studies at the Society's school, Payne became a private student of Thomas S. Bonneau, a prominent educator in Charleston, for three additional years.[10] Apparently, the love of learning captured him during these formal years of schooling and being tutored. He read voraciously, was exposed to the popular histories of the period, and acquired the requisite writing and speaking skills for being an educator. This pattern of learning was so ingrained in the youngster that from twelve years of age when he apprenticed at a carpenter's store, helped in a tailoring store, and worked in shoe repair shop, Payne continued to read on his own.[11] Part of this self-discipline can be attributed to a short biography of the cleric, John Brown of Haddington, Scotland included at the beginning of the *Self-Interpreting Bible* which Payne read during this period.

Payne's mention of this biographical sketch is important from two perspectives. First, Payne as a young teen could identify with Brown whose parents died by the time he was eleven years of age. Second, Brown had very little formal education except for the basic components of reading, writing, and arithmetic which were available to the lower classes of Scotland. Third, Brown, who became interested in a theological education through his encounter with clergy from the Church of Scotland, learned Latin, Greek, and Hebrew on his own. He accomplished this after working or during his breaks as work.[12] If Brown had learned Latin, Greek, and Hebrew without the aid of a teacher, Payne, inspired by that description, vowed to do the same and read even more feverishly.

When at age eighteen he described his conversion experience, there soon followed a prayerful session when he heard the words of someone state, "I have set thee apart to educate thyself in order that thou mayest be an educator to thy people" which he described as "irresistible and divine."[13] He acquired money for books through his ability to do carpentry where he sold his products at the public market. He read at every possible free moment in the work day. However modest or lucrative his income, the call to be the educator outweighed his ability and gifts as a craftsman and so at age nineteen, Payne left the world of carpentry and began the life of the educator opening his first school in 1829.

While I contend, and Payne's own words confirm, that the educational affinity of Payne can be attributed to his parents and the church, his educational attainment and interest were developed in the context of South Carolina, in the early nineteenth century. It is important to note the fact of free persons of color in South Carolina, as well as the educational opportunities which were opened to them during this national or expanding period of education in the United States.

Charleston, South Carolina was a commercial center for the region. Bernard Powers, in *Black Charlestonians,* notes that Charleston was a city second only to Baltimore, Maryland in terms of commercial prominence in the early nineteenth century.[14] In addition to its strong economic base, it served as a cultural center for the southern planters who basked in luxury with good restaurants, theater, and sports areas. But more importantly for this study, one notes the large black population that existed. In fact, blacks outnumbered whites in seven of the eight decades between 1780 and 1860. They were a very visible presence, with slave involvement in various occupations including "bricklayers, blacksmiths, carpenters, tailors, bakers, plasterers, coopers, shoemakers, and miscellaneous mechanical trades for men" and needlecrafts for women.[15] In relationship to this city which was situated along coastal waters, slaves were also involved in maritime occupations such as wharf hands and stevedores, and were working hands on steamboats and sloops.[16]

The blacks in Charleston included both slaves and free persons of color. In fact, there was a significant free black population throughout the state. Although this free status put most of them on the lowest level of the society, some acquired property, in some cases slaves, and created their own social institutions. Powers notes, however, "...the quality and character of their lives was conditioned by the stark reality of existence within a slaveholding society."[17] This community developed in the late seventeenth century and by 1850 there were 3441 free persons.[18] The demographics of this population indicate that by 1850, seventy-five percent of this group were mulattoes, the children of slaveholders, while the slave population consisted of eight percent mulattoes.[19] The majority of the free blacks were involved in skilled or semi-skilled employment by the mid-nineteenth century.[20]

Socially, this group of blacks maintained a sense of familial identity and most often married other free persons of color. This sense of family was exhibited in their guarded genealogies and records of important events in the family, including the occurrences of births, illnesses, and deaths of family members.[21] There were some family names which were known and with whom Payne was acquainted, including the Holloways and Bonneaus. As mentioned previously, Payne studied with Thomas Bonneau who was a prominent free black teacher. While they worked to maintain their social status, they demonstrated their concern for the education of black children. From this group of free black came the organizers who formed and operated the Minor's Moralist school which Payne attended. Each of its members paid an entrance fee of five dollars and monthly dues of twenty-five cents. In addition to the above families, the school was also supported by other prominent free blacks.[22]

It must also be noted that an additional avenue for the education of the free black came from the gathering of the community in churches. The Cumberland Street Methodist Church had a Sunday school which was one of the oldest established for and under the leadership of free blacks.[23] Payne was a member and teacher there along with other prominent persons of color in the Charleston community. What was the plight of the free Black? However different the lives of these free blacks look in contrast to their slave brothers and sisters, and while we might imagine their living conditions to be better, researchers remind us that they were not as free as the term implies. Powers reminds us,

It was also the whites' shared notion of a society predicated upon the degradation of all Afro-Americans that brought the interests of slaves and most free blacks closer together. Some free blacks enjoyed privileges, but they were the exception. Moreover, free blacks were identified with the enslaved group by a common racial heritage and were made to share in the slaves' degradation at every turn. Free persons of color were tried in slave courts along with their fettered brethren and likewise were subject to the arbitrary justice of the slave patrol.[24]

With the rise of slave insurrections, most notably from the Demark Vesey conspiracy, additional limitations were put on slaves as well as free persons of color. Demark Vesey, a carpenter in Charleston, South Carolina, had used his religious and secular education to pave the way for freedom. Thus, education of any slave or free persons of color was seen as a threat to the majority. Powers notes that, "...in 1822 [the year of the Vesey conspiracy], free persons of color were required to register twice a year with the attendant and to explain any prolonged period of absence from the city. That same year, the Charleston delegation introduced a bill to the legislature to banish all free blacks who had come to the state in the previous five years.[25]

In spite of the opposition, limitations, and suspicions which were placed on all people of color, slave or free, regarding education or freedom in the United States, Payne still felt called to be the educator. We see it in the educational experiences which were offered to him, his own self-education, and his commitment to the education of children and adults of color. From these experiences and commitments Payne opened his first school in 1829 in the home of a Caesar Wright whose three children were his students. Payne also taught three slave adults at night and received from each a total of fifty cents each. The low rate of reimbursement and the need to survive caused him to consider other sources of income and abandon the teaching field and close the school.

The opportunity for other employment came to Payne when a slave-holder wanted a free person of color to work for his business. When Payne was engaged in the interview, he recalled an important juncture in the conversation when the owner commented, "If you will go with me, the knowledge that you will acquire of men and things will be of far more value to you than the wages I will pay you." He further questioned Payne, "Do you know what makes the difference between the master and the slave? Nothing but superior knowledge."[26] Payne quickly reflected on these words and said to himself, "If it is true that there is nothing but superior knowledge between the master and the slave, I will not go with you but will rather go and obtain that knowledge which constitutes the master."[27]

Payne returned to reopen his school and continued to teach. He was very successful at this second educational venture and many of the citizenry were amazed at the quality of the students and the curriculum to which the students were exposed. With the reopening of the school, Payne became the passionate teacher; the teacher who was dedicated to the art and science of transmitting knowledge to the next generation of young boys and girls of color. He described this dedication with the following, "My enthusiasm was the inspiration of my students."[28]

As much as the words reveal his zeal for teaching his students, another important component to this dedication and the glue which reinforces his personal goals in education was his use of textbooks. Payne remembered the texts, and this gives us an indication of his theory and theology of education. An analysis of each of the texts used is helpful to us. While we do not have a formal curriculum placed before us with the scope and sequence of the courses, we do have a picture of his expectations for preparing boys and girls of color for life in nineteenth century United States.

Payne was an effective communicator and expected his students to communicate with standard patterns of the English language. To this end, Payne used one of the popular English grammar books of the period, Lindley Murray's *English Grammar Adapted to the Different Classes of Learners*.[29] More than the memorization of rules of grammar, the objective of the text was to develop what might be called formal operational thought or critical thinking skills of students. The author commented that the textbook also had the goal "[of inviting] the ingenious student to inquiry and reflection, and to prompt to (sic) a more enlarged, critical, and philosophical research."[30] Payne's use of this text might be attributed to deliberate sensitivity to the various learners in the United States classrooms during this early period in the nation's educational formation. William F. Wood states that the phrase "different classes of learners," in the title indicated the reality of the one-room school house in which included students from the early grades through high school preparing to enter college. To accommodate the various ages and abilities in the classroom Murray's text included: different print sizes so that younger students were able to learn the general principles of grammar by reading the large print sections of the chapters and advanced students were given expanded information and examples by reading the small print, memorization exercises were designed to "form the mind," and the textbook could be used by those students attending formal classes as well as by those students, particularly those who were older and beyond school age, who studied on their own at their own pace.[31]

Payne also studied and introduced geometry to his students. He prepared himself by using an edition of John Playfair's *Elements of Geometry containing the First Six Books of Euclid*.[32] Again, the objective of Payne was to serve the student by developing the mind of the students to think critically as well as to broaden the curriculum which was usually watered down or minimal at most to children of color. Payne's objective was consistent with the objectives of Playfair who wrote in the preface:

> To all this it may be added, that the mind, especially when beginning to study the art of reasoning, cannot be employed to greater advantage than in analysing those judgments, which, though they appear simple, are in reality complex, and capable of being distinguished into parts. No progress in ascending higher can be expected, till a regular habit of demonstration is thus acquired; it is much to be feared, that he who has declined the trouble of tracing the connection be-

tween the proposition already quoted, and those that are more simple, will not be very expert in tracing its connection with those that are more complex; and that, as he has not been careful in laying the foundation, he will never be successful in raising the superstructure.[33]

The curriculum of the school also included chemistry, natural philosophy,[34] and descriptive chemistry. Payne even utilized Burritt's, *The Geography of the Heavens*.[35] Again, the objective of the text was congruent with Payne's objective and experience as a teacher. It was the intention of Burritt to have a book which would assist students in not only memorize the solar system but also to view and comprehend according to their adolescent ability with the use of "familiar lesson, exercises, and illustrations."[36] In addition, Burritt stated that in order for this to take place, he had not relied on books, maps or globes. Rather, "I came, at length, to the conclusion, that any description of the stars, to be practically useful, must be made from a careful observation of the stars themselves, and made at the time of the observation."[37] He also pointed out that this subject had not been an important component of the curriculum, therefore, this text would assist students in knowing what they were viewing in the sky. Furthermore, the study of the sky was not to undermine Christian belief system, but just the opposite, to have the ability to support that belief system.

His students were given introductory lessons to the mathematic sciences and Payne was appreciative of the fundamentals available to him as teacher and to his students as learners. These fundamentals influenced him to examine the larger curriculum landscape of his school for he even used the term "superstructure" when commenting on his personal goals for the school, "Having now the groundwork, I began to build the superstructure."[38]

Payne's work on course offerings would develop the curriculum for the students, but also to explore the educational interests and goals of the teacher himself. Payne exposed himself to languages: Greek, Latin, and French and to the arts and sciences: botany and zoology.[39] His interest in teaching the subjects to his students gave him the opportunity to meet and observe the work of Dr. John Bachman, the distinguished naturalist who was also the pastor of St. John's Lutheran Church.[40] In preparing to teach his students, Payne was not able to identify a particular species of a worm. He was directed to make contact with Bachman who received him warmly and helped Payne to identify the worm, its habits, and the stage of its development. This encounter that Payne had with Bachman was significant in two ways. First, Payne begins a friendship with Bachman and thus his initial encounter with Lutheran Christians which will play an important role in Payne's professional development. Second, though Bachman was a supporter of slavery yet he was open to conversations with Payne. Raymond Bost notes that "In relation to slavery,

Bachman was one of the South's prominent defenders of the institution as sanctioned in the Bible. As a scientist, however, he opposed such prominent scientific personages as Louis Agassiz, by arguing the Negro and white men were of the same species."[41] Bachman's scientific leanings were confirmed by Payne when he reflected on another visit he made to Bachman, "I sat and conversed with his family as freely as though all were of the same color and equal rank..."[42]

However enthusiastic Payne was as a teacher, new state legislation as well as rumors of the success of his school forced the school to close in the spring of 1835. The state General Assembly approved a law which prohibited the education of black slaves by whites or blacks. The law stated,

> If any person shall hereafter teach any slave to read or write, or cause, or procure any slave to read or write, such person, if a free white person upon conviction thereof shall for each and every offense against this Act be fined not exceeding one hundred dollars and imprisoned not more than six months; or, if a free person of color, shall be whipped not exceeding fifty lashes and fined not exceeding fifty dollars...and if a slave, to be whipped at the discretion of the court, not exceeding fifty lashes[43]

At the time of the closing of the school, the enrollment had increased and was the largest of the five schools in the area with about 60 students according to Payne.[44] Payne also noted the rumors that certainly were unfounded about the success of his students. Some observers thought that he must have dealt in sorcery. Moreover, some felt that the curriculum he designed was the course of study designed by someone who had been trained in a college which was not the case.

March 31, 1835 marked the closing of the school doors and the beginning of a long journey and hiatus away from the place of his birth. It was the death nail for any aspiration of being the teacher called to educate his brothers and sisters of color. This was the most difficult period for him vocationally and religiously. But, wasn't he called to this work? It was his vocation, was it not? What tricks was God playing with him? It is during this period that Payne wrote one of his most poignant passages:

> Sometimes it seems as though some wild beast had plunged his fangs into my heart, and was squeezing out its life-blood. Then I began to question the existence of God, and to say: "If he does exist, is he just? If so, why does he suffer one race to oppress and enslave another, to rob them by unrighteous enactments of rights, which they hold most dear and sacred?...Again said I: "Is there no God?"[45]

In a sense these words echo the cries of the Psalms and those of the Prophets. Payne could not understand the reasons for subjugation of men and women of color, his brothers and sisters. But in the end, he is comforted by the words, "With God one day is as a thousand years and a thousand years as one day. Trust in him and he will bring slavery and all its outrages to an end."[46] Thus Payne put his trust in the one who had led him to this point in his life. This God would not abandon him. In response to his anger, questioning and ultimate relief from this turmoil, Payne composed the poem, "The Mournful Lute, or the Preceptor's Farewell." Selected verses reflect the agony and hope of this teacher:

> Pupils, attend my last departing sounds;
> Ye are my hopes, and my mental crowns,
> My monuments of intellectual might,
> My robes of honor and my armor bright.
> Like Solomon, entreat the throne of God;
> Light shall descend in lucid columns broad,
> And all that man has learned or man can know
> In streams prolific shall your minds o'erflow.
>
> Hate sin; love God; religion be your prize;
> Her laws obeyed will surely make you wise,
> Secure you from the ruin of the vain,
> And save your souls from everlasting pain.
> O fare you well for whom my bosom glows
> With ardent love, which Christ my Saviour knows?
> 'Twas for your good I labored night and day;
> For you I wept, and now for you I pray.
> Farewell! Farewell! Ye children of my love;
> May joys abundant flow ye from above!
> May peace celestial crown your useful days,
> To bliss transported, sing eternal lays;
> From sacred wisdom give a golden world,
> And when foul vice his charming folds unfurl,
> O spurn the monster, though his crystal eyes
> Be like bright sunbeams streaming from the skies!
> And I! O whither shall your tutor fly?
> Guide thou my feet, great Sovereign in the sky.
> A useful life by sacred wisdom crowned,
> Is all I ask, let weal or woe abound![47]

THE ROAD TO GETTYSBURG

After writing these words and facing the inevitable closing of the school, Payne experienced a dream in which he did not remain in Charleston but traveled to the northern states and was dressed in a teaching garment. This dream appeared to have helped him for upon waking, he decided to travel north where he would be able to continue to educate young boys and girls without obstacles in his way. With that decision he made visits to various acquaintances for references and letters of introduction.[48] The two persons who stand out from this list were Dr. John Bachman and Mr. Samuel Weston, the latter a class leader in the Methodist Episcopal Church where Payne attended. Payne described him as "venerable, intelligent, holy man."[49] He was not able to progress beyond that because of the perception of the majority population that he was a black man and less than whole. He would become a "mentor." From Dr. Bachman Payne was able to make introductions in northern Lutheran circles. In general the letters certainly would be helpful in giving the young teacher hope for a new beginning in the north. Clearly, Payne took encouragement from their letters.

Dr. Bachman's note included the following comments:

A mysterious providence has so ordered it that your usefulness in the profession you have chosen is at an end in your native city...

Carry; with you this parting advice from one who entertains a favorable opinion of your acquirements and worth: Pursue knowledge wherever it is to be found. Like the air you breathe, it may be inhaled everywhere; like gold, it passes current among all classes. Perform all your duties faithfully...[50]

The letter from Dr. Palmer indicated his view of the now banished teacher:

...Bear on your heart wherever you go your colored brethren on whom the light of hope begins auspiciously to dawn. As further light shines on your own bewildered path, let its reflection illumine theirs...Let your future purposes and pursuits all bear favorably and strongly toward the accomplishment of the interesting, the divine assurance, "Ethiopia shall soon stretch out her hand to God" My he who gave this promise be ever with you![51]

With his letters of introduction, belongings packed, tears, emotional pangs, and deep regret, yet, simultaneously, trusting in God's promise to be with him, Daniel sailed from Charleston in the late afternoon of 9 May1935 for New York City. The goal for this voyage was to be the teacher to his brothers and sisters of color.[52] As the ship sailed up the coastal waters of the eastern United States, it was impossible to know or envision the experiences, encounters, and tasks upon which he was going to embark. Upon his arrival at the port of New York, Payne settled in at a boarding house and began to make use of his letters of introduction.

He went to the Rev. Peter Williams, a clergyman of color of the Protestant Episcopal Church, who did not have any suggestions for him at the time and to officers of the Methodist Book Concern but their recommendation was to go to Africa. Payne was not interested in such a venture for he felt his call to serve within the United States.[53] In the midst of this visit to New York, he also attended an anti-slavery meeting where he heard George Thompson speak against the institution of slavery. He also encountered Lewis Tappan who was speaking in support of an educational tract entitled, *Child's Anti-Slavery Magazine* which he deemed to be helpful to the next generation of citizens.[54]

Payne's final visit of introduction in New York was to Pastor Strobel, a Lutheran, to whom Payne gave a letter from Dr. Bachman. Bachman was a mentor of Strobel who shared with Payne that he had arrived at a fortunate time for he had just been informed by a Dr. Martin that there was a scholarship which was being offered by the student group, "The Society of Inquiry on Missions." They intended to provide a scholarship for a young man of color who demonstrated talent and piety in order for that person to help with the social uplift of his people. Strobel felt that Daniel Payne was just the type of person who would be eligible for the scholarship. Strobel stated further "Now, if you will go to Gettysburg and study theology there, you will be better fitted than you now are for usefulness among your people."[55]

Pastor Strobel's importance merits an introduction as a key figure. Pastor Strobel was born in Charleston, South Carolina in 1808 and studied theology under the tutelage of Dr. John Bachman in South Carolina. He was licensed in 1829 by the New York Ministerium and ordained by the South Carolina Synod in 1830. He was assigned as a missionary to work in some of the counties in the South Carolina. He left from the area in 1831 when he transferred to work in New York City. His domestic missionary work would have made him well acquainted with the various missionary activities of the Lutheran Church.[56] His knowledge of the scholarship came from Strobel's correspondence with Dr. Martin. Martin had received an M.D. degree from the University of Pennsylvania and immediately studied theology at Gettysburg Seminary. At the time of Strobel's conversation with Payne, Martin was a seminarian and a member of the Society.[57]

The Society of Inquiry on Missions was a student group across the collegiate campuses in the United States which was popular during the first half of the nineteenth century. Coan notes that its objectives included: to cultivate the devotional life, informing students about mission issues, and to sponsor student activities such as providing education for a student for service in the Church.[58] The students at Andover Seminary were catalysts in promoting and maintaining correspondence of the Society with their peers at other institutions.

The Evangelical Lutheran Society of Inquiry on Missions was established at Gettysburg Seminary in February 1827. The Society's objectives were to help prepare these men for the task of ministry upon leaving seminary and to acquaint them with the various world religions. To these ends the students would present papers for discussion, review works dedicated to missions, and examine the lives of missionaries at their regular meetings.[59] The call to service was concretized with their decision to support a person of color with a scholarship to study theology at their school. The minutes of a regular meeting of the society on March 4, 1835, indicated that the membership pledged to support a free person of color for theological education:

> Resolved that the members of this Society pledge themselves to afford a support to a suitable, free coloured man (if such a one can be obtained) sufficient to enable him to employ four years, in this seminary, in the prosecution of studies preparatory, to the sacred ministry, in the Lutheran Church...[60]

Although Pastor Strobel offered Payne the opportunity to accept the scholarship offer, Payne did not immediately give a positive response because of several issues important to him. He was reluctant to seize this opportunity because his goal and passion centered on teaching. Theology was not part of that agenda or even on the path for meeting the objective of teaching. He did not see himself as a likely candidate for ordained ministry. Strobel responded to this ambivalence by stating to Payne that theology might better prepare him for the task of teaching and that Payne's students would benefit with his knowledge of theology. Payne left to think about the offer.

Payne returned to his lodging and began to acquaint himself with the doctrines of the Lutheran Church. To that end, he read Samuel Simon Schmucker's *Unabridged Popular Theology*. He was struck by Schmucker's writing. Schmucker was the president of Gettysburg Seminary, and his theological work had been published the previous year. The author hoped that this text would be seen as a "prayerful effort to render the work instructive and edifying to the intelligent Christian and theological student..."[61] While Payne was affected by the scholarship it appears that he was also impressed by Schmucker's commitment to abolition. In the section "Emancipation," Schmucker cited the words of the Declaration of Independence. When governments were not dedicated to the equality of all men, the populace had the responsibility to take arms. He argued that this was ironic in light of the plight of the enslaved African.[62] Schmucker went on to say that although he supported the Colonization Society from its inception, nevertheless, he realized that not all Africans would return to the African continent, for many would find it to be an unknown place.

Moreover, Schmucker's passionate stance must have struck Payne when he read the following words:

> All should feel that crying injustice was inflicted by our ancestors on the poor African, by reducing him to slavery, and that we become partakers of their guilt, if we protract his degradation, and delay his restoration to the unalienable rights of man. Let the American patriot recollect the language of his fathers, "that all men are created equal," and have unalienable rights, among which is "liberty." Let him remember, that with these words on their lips, they invoked the blessing of Heaven on their struggle, and that He who rules in the heaven of heavens heard their cry. Then let him look at the poor African, doomed to drag out his life in slavery amidst us.[63]

Such strong advocacy must have caused Payne to reconsider his call in life. He began to ponder the idea of attending Gettysburg and writing "I would there be in the hands of a teacher who would be as liberal as he was Christian and learned."[64] When Payne returned to speak with Pastor Strobel, Payne had two questions to present which would really make or break his decision to attend the seminary. The first question had to do with any requirement that he become a Lutheran in order to receive this educational opportunity. Strobel responded in the negative. The second undoubtedly came from his reading Schmucker's work. The second question was whether he would be expected to sent to Africa at the end of his study. Payne noted that the African colonization movement went against the American Anti-Slavery Society Again, Strobel responded in the negative. His responses confirmed what Payne had decided to do, and he set out for Gettysburg, Pennsylvania after a few days more in New York City meeting and visiting with more people.

Among his visits Payne noted several in particular. Peter Williams was a clergyman in the Methodist Church. This particular person stood out to Payne as a lover of education who supported young people pursuing studies. He was also an advocate of an educated clergy. Mr. Thomas B. Downing was a person of color, a business man who owned a restaurant on Wall Street, and was an abolitionist. Payne also visited Thomas Hamilton, whose son was a publisher of the *Anglo-African* and Mr. Charles Reason who was a public school educator and benefactor to education.

In addition, Payne met the Rev. Charles B. Ray who was a missionary to the city, a Congregational pastor and a founder of the *Colored American*. Payne noted that this was the only weekly journal edited by persons of color.[65] Payne also noted the accomplishments of his children: three females who were educated at home as well as in the New York public schools.

One visit was of particular value as one traces a theme of liberation in education. A visit with Lewis Tappan, the New York lawyer, assisted in Payne's transformation regarding slavery, education and the process for liberation. Payne wrote,

> Immediately he began to interrogate me concerning slavery as it had manifested itself in my native city, and concluded his inquiries by asking me what I thought of "immediate and unconditional emancipation." I replied that I was opposed to that, because I believed the slaves ought to be educated before emancipation, that they might know how to enjoy freedom. Instantly he replied: "Don't you know that men can't be educated in a state of slavery?" He then convinced me in a few words that education and slavery were antagonistic and could not exist together—that the one must crush out the other.[66]

While this process was an important revelation to Payne, it also made him aware of the role and the attitude of the abolitionists of his day. He commented that his mind was changed with this brief encounter. Having come from South Carolina, a community and environment which saw the abolitionist as an agitator, he saw and heard for himself the dedication and commitment of a gentleman like Tappen and others like him to the liberation of Payne's bound brothers and sisters. Payne was impressed by Tappan because he was a prayerful man and so could not be a bad person.[67] From New York, his next stop on his way to Gettysburg was in the city of Philadelphia where he met other notable persons. These encounters included the Rev. Samuel Cornish, a Presbyterian pastor who founded Shiloh Presbyterian Church. Cornish's two brothers, William and John, were elders in the in A.M.E.Church. He also met George S. Downing, Esquire who was a voice for human rights on behalf of the Black citizens of the United States.[68]

Among his other contacts was a person of color, Joseph Cassey, a prominent and wealthy manufacturer of beauty products for the hair. He also encountered the Forten and Purvis families. The Fortens had eight children. He commented that they were all talented, but that his son Robert was a gifted mathematician, optician, and poet. Robert Purvis, a person of color, active in the Anti-Slavery movement, had been president of the American Anti-Slavery Society, president of the Pennsylvania Anti-Slavery Society, and president of the Under-ground Railroad Society.[69]

GETTYSBURG SEMINARY

After his short stay in what he called the "Quaker City," Payne took the train from Philadelphia to Columbia, Pennsylvania. There he transferred to stage coach and arrived in the rural town of Gettysburg in the south central part of the state. Arriving in the month of June, he was able to see the farmers and their helpers taking care of the fields. Exhausted from the trip he was able to get a room in a hotel and rested until the next day when he reached the steps of the seminary. Payne's life had been transformed in the space of four weeks. While he admired the beauty of the Blue Mountains and the flow of the hills from the point of the seminary, he could not get the image of his school and the students he taught out of his mind. On the one hand, he was experiencing beauty and peace; yet, on the other hand, this came through unjust actions on the part of the state government. He missed his home and his work. But his words express it best,

> ...O the parting scene in that school-room, those interesting children, and my sister, my only sister, whom I would never see again! But what made my thought almost agonizing was the recollection of the fact that this separation was the bitter product of unjust, cruel, and blasphemous laws—cruel and unjust to a defenseless race, blasphemous of that God who of one blood did make all the nations of the earth, all its races, all its families, every individual. Every night for many years after I left Charleston did I dream about it—wandering over its streets, bathing in its rivers, worshiping in its chapels, or teaching in my school-room, and sometimes I was sailing into it and sometimes flying out of it.[70]

This was not a pain that was going to go away quickly. He was cut off from his family, friends, livelihood, and his roots. That separation which he experienced with this brief departure from Charleston would haunt him for a few years to come.

Payne's life at Gettysburg was in some ways like other students pursuing the study of theology for church leadership. He was enrolled for the July session. The curriculum for the three year program of the seminary included: Greek Philology, Hebrew Philology, Sacred Geography, Sacred Chronology, Biblical and Profane History Connected, Biblical Antiquities in the first or Junior year; Philosophy of the Mind, Natural Theology, Evidences of Christianity, Biblical Criticism, Exegetical Theology, Biblical Theology, Systematic Divinity, Practical Divinity, and Ecclesiastical History in the second or Middle year; Ecclesiastical History, Polemic Theology, Practical Divinity, Church Government, Composition and Delivery of Sermons, Pastoral Theology in the senior year.[71] Although the course of study was designed for three years most students did not complete the three years of study nor were all the courses offered.[72]

In addition to his theological studies, Payne also engaged himself in the life of a seminary student. He was an active member of the "Evangelical Lutheran Society of Inquiry on Missions," the student group which had awarded him the scholarship. The Society's meetings consisted of the reading of correspondence from former students, now in the missionary field both domestic and foreign. In addition, students read and heard papers from their own inquiry on a particular topic consistent with this area of ministry as well as discussed general concerns. At Gettysburg, the documentary evidence indicates that it was not unusual for Dr. Schmucker to attend these meetings and listen to the presentations or share his particular concerns. Moreover, the students would correspond with their peers at other seminaries in the country. In fact, they shared their scholarship project with the fellow seminarians at the Lutheran Seminary in Columbia, South Carolina. The June correspondence from the secretary stated,

> Rev. Mr. Bachman of your state has been elected Pres. of the Synod. This missionary society of our seminary have (sic) under these days D. A. Payne a coloured man recently of S. Carolina (Charleston)whom we are educating for the ministry of the gospel, at our last meeting we resolved to support a young man of colour till he should be qualified to preach the gospel, we have every reason to believe that Providence has directed him hither and we pray that he may be made abundantly useful enlightening and evangelizing the children of Africa in our country, too long have they been kept in ignorance, too long have they had pointed at them the fringing scorn, it is high time that Americas awake they have published it to the world that all men are created equal, that they are endowed by the Creator with certain unalienable rights, but they have not put into practice the truth which is self evident. We are not in favor of immediate abolition, but do think that we dare not pursue this course which has heretofore been the acknowledged, the lawful one....Wm. N. Sholl, Cor.Secty.[73]

This group took primary responsibility for financing his education at Gettysburg. A student committee from the Society was formed to arrange for Payne's room, board, and transportation while at Gettysburg.[74] Payne participated in the group, from presenting papers to his peers to saying the closing prayer at the conclusion of the meeting.[75] There were times when the group discussed the issue of slavery in the States. Needless to say, the students were abolitionists in their thinking and questioned the issue on theological and political grounds. All we can assume is that they continued their stance while Payne was a student as noted in a few fragments of commentary from the recorder of the minutes:

> ...Dr. Martin presented to the Society, from A. Tappan New York, ...inquiry into the merits of the American Colonization and Anti-Slavery Societies, also 5 miscellaneous pamphlets, which were accepted, and on motion Resolved that the thanks of the Society be presented to Mr. Tappan, whenever an opportunity is afforded to any one of the students.[76]

There appeared to be four viewpoints examined by the students around the slavery issue: The first, those who feel that the institution of slavery had a scriptural and political support. This viewpoint was supported by those ben-efitting economically from the institution, slave-holders and dealers. Coloni-zation is the second view which advocates the emancipation of all slaves and their return to the African continent. This view is reported to be supported by Society of Quakers. The third view advocates the liberation of the slave at a time which would benefit both white and black people; "...many of wisest and best" support this view the secretary wrote. Abolition is the fourth view. The supporters of this view advocated the immediate and unconditional liberation of slaves. This view is particularly noted in the North and non-slave-holding states. This view gained momentum as the number of abolitionist societies increased. In summary the discussion ends with the following, "It is our prayer that God may overrule all these conflicting opinions, that good may be brought out of evil and that [ ] the wrath of man many be made to praise him."[77]

In addition, to this extracurricular activity, Payne also availed himself of the opportunity to preach in nearby churches and mission points, to teach Sunday school, and to devote himself to private devotions.[78] In the midst of these activities Payne made several transformations. First, after being at the seminary for three months, he was confirmed into the Lutheran Church and then participated in the eucharist. Second, he made connections with Bethel the AME Church in Carlisle, Pennsylvania. Third, he becomes introspective and develops a stronger piety than was exhibited prior to coming to the semi-nary. Payne gave no explanation for this religious transformation or the pro-cess of catechesis. His only comment on the night before his confirmation, "O my God, I earnestly pray thee, to prepare my heart for the enjoyment of the same. O give me thy spirit."[79] But Payne must have felt he was theologically at home. Payne saw it demonstrated in the integration of theological acuity and living the Christian life, particularly illustrated in the life of President Schmucker who was both a pietist and an abolitionist. That was reflected in his writings as well in his impact on the thinking of the students under his care as President of Gettysburg Seminary.

The pietist movement is rooted in seventeenth century Germany. Spe-cifically, scholars have attributed the movement to the publication of Philipp Jakob Spener's work *Pia Desideria* which was published in 1675. The move-ment's adherents expressed themselves in exhibiting a deliberate and con-scious relationship to God. This new relationship was expressed in a visible change in lifestyle with a life expressive of the love of God. Denominational identity was diminished and the common identity as "brother" and "sister," as they called each other took precedence over race, class, and nationality.[80] The important components of pietism included: a strong devotional life, focus on the sermon in worship life of the community, strong social ministry concerns, emphasis on ethical and religious identity of the pastor, and emphasis on missionary activities. Pietism's Lutheran presence came to America through the work of Henry Melchior Muhlenberg in the mid-eighteenth century as a missionary to the United States from Germany. Schmucker inherited the tradition, and it was exhibited in the admission policies, curriculum, and extracurricular activities during Payne's years at Gettysburg Seminary.

Schmucker's inaugural address as President of Gettysburg Seminary entitled, "The Theological Education of Ministers," identified two prerequisites for the theological student of quality, "fervent piety and good natural talents."[81] For Schmucker, piety was a requirement; for without it, the man could not be faithful minister and would be a hindrance to the mission of church and to himself. In the case of natural talents, Schmucker was not requiring an erudite student of superior intelligence but a student who would be able to have sound judgement. Thus he states: "The men, therefore, who are best qualified for the study of theology, are those who are possessed of at least mediocrity of mind, men of prudent deportment, men born of the spirit."[82] The ideal theological student demonstrated a love for God and a capacity for exhibiting that love in acts of mercy. In addition, the student would have those abilities which would benefit his future congregants. Within the curriculum, pietists influenced the theological curriculum with their stress on biblical interpretation and individual devotional reading of the scriptures. In the published curriculum, the middle or second year of studies included a course in Biblical Theology in addition to courses in Biblical Criticism and Exegetical Theology.[83] The Inaugural also included Schmucker's advocacy of "searching the scripture with knowledge of Greek and Hebrew philology, interpretation, Biblical Archeology, Practical and Pastoral Theology, Government and Discipline as well.[84] The influence of the Pietism within the theological education at Gettysburg was also demonstrated in the Evangelical Lutheran Society of Inquiry on Missions which supported Payne and to which, as was mentioned above, he was a participating member. The students and the program were centered on showing and encouraging a visible piety. One example of this concern occurred at a meeting in which President Schmucker was present. Schmucker recommended that a student committee be formed in order to examine the status of the churches in Eastern Pennsylvania. Apparently, there was a need to develop a strategy for improving the "state of piety" for churches in that area.[85] Moreover, the Society in its "Preamble" supported the missionary efforts which were taking place in the areas of the land and world where there was a need for conversion of "the heathen" (sic) to the knowledge and service of the one true God. To all this, Schmucker also was emphatic about an educated, learned clergy in the church. To practice one's devotion and allegiance to God was not an excuse for anti-intellectual activity or neglect of continuing, on-going education of the student. Schmucker was emphatic when he stated, "...[A] religion that is from God, will not shrink from investigation, nor tremble before the intellectual attitude of friends or foes."[86]

To all this Payne was more than able to identify and participate as a member of the student body. His demonstrated piety can be documented in his diary entries. On one entry Payne resolved to go to bed early and rise by 4:00 AM in order to have personal prayer, read the Bible and take time for meditation. This would be repeated after dinner and before retiring for the evening.[87]

For all the benefits of being a student, with the opportunity to continue his life of learning, reading, and teaching through his theological studies, one issue continued to be with him, that is to say, isolation. After a half a year on the Gettysburg campus, Payne records on his twenty-fifth birthday:

This day last year I was home amidst a large circle of friends surrounded by numerous lovely pupils. But today where am I? More than 600 miles from the place of my nativity. Among strangers, among benefactors, but not among friends in the strict sense of that word. For a friend is one to whom we can unbosom our most secret thoughts. But I look in vain for such a one here. Oh! My friends, my friends! My dear friends where are you now? But enough of this Lord I have enough to make me grateful, O make me contented. Ah, here is a sweet Reflection (sic), that though I am far from my friends and Relatives (sic) I have the esteem and Christian kindness of the wise, the great and the good. I have the only object of my heart desires of an earthly nature, or that the chief one is that of acquiring knowledge and of being useful among my oppressed despised and ignorant brethren.[88]

In addition to his studies and devotions, Payne also took advantage of the opportunities to preach and teach in the area. His diary entries exhibit his continued interest in teaching through the Sunday schools locally in Gettysburg and in the neighboring town of Carlisle. His continued interest in religious education prompted him to establish a Sunday school for Black children in Gettysburg. He used an old building on the grounds of Gettysburg College and used townspeople as well as his fellow seminarians as teachers.[89] Moreover, his involvement in the formation of the Society for Moral and Mental Improvement and his lectures on grammar and geography kept him occupied.[90] He doesn't describe the development of his homiletical interests and ability but he does accept requests to preach in congregations. Time was also spent with visitations to the sick and the American Anti-slavery meetings.[91] With all the extra-curricular and church-related involvement, Payne took on odd jobs to supplement his scholarship including chopping wood, cleaning shoes and boots, and cutting hair. These involvements would seem to keep anyone occupied to the point of exhaustion, but it appears that Payne thrived.

At the same time we see someone searching for equilibrium in his religious development. Although he embraced the ecclesia and educational structures of the Lutheran Church, one finds the theological underpinnings of his Methodist roots surface in the intimate moments of his daily reflections in his diary. He still is not settled within himself and one sees bouts of angst exhibited in his journal:

> Saturday Night, June 25, 1836
> Yes, my Saviour, I have not lived this week as it behooves me to live. O, do thou forgive me, and may my heart henceforth bear a perpetual accord with thy Sacred Words. It does seem strange that I who know they will so well and who studies thy word daily should indulge in such fits of levity.

> June 28, 1836
> Another day have I spent in bareness, but out from the light of God's countenance. O, My soul! My soul where art thou? With, O Wither art thou wandering? Saviour come to my rescue! Accursed levity, how hast thou robbed me of my sacred communion with my Almighty Sovereign...

> Saturday night, January 28
> I have thought and said many things this week which have been more or less vain and sinful. And thought at other times I have endeavored to walk with the Lord. Yet I feel that found wanting last night. Thus imperfect are all attempts to worship God! How little do I love thee, I, thou Holy One of Israel!

> Friday morning early, March 25, 1837
> Yesterday I fell into sin and grieved the Holy Spirit. I have departed for the path of Righteousness. O, Lord, have mercy upon me, and pardon me for the Redeemer's Sake, O, for his suffering, our forgiver, forgive me, a miserable offender, the most ungrateful and unfaithful of all that ever received they Grace.[92]

What incidents or which persons prompted these bouts of anguish, sadness, and self-deprecation? Payne does not give the details. We can only guess. To some extent, although he was immersed into the life of the seminary and the community, Payne was still in foreign territory. He was away from family and close friends, venturing on his own. At the same time, one might see in these emotional entries that the vocation was not only an intellectual idea or dream, but an immersion and submission to the will of God which would override any self-gratification. In a more pointed way, the venture to Gettysburg was a radical transformation for him. Payne agreed to accept the scholarship to come to Gettysburg because he would not be required to change his denominational affiliation nor have to become a divine. After only two months, he was confirmed and then one sees him engaged in preaching in addition to continuing his interests in religious and general education. Although Payne did not explicitly indicate one particular factor, he was in an environment which was racially isolated compared to the large Black population of Charleston, South Carolina. This also contributed to his isolation. His various activities in the region rather then restricting himself to the town of Gettysburg, helped to bridge the gap between his theological studies and his social interaction with other people of color as there were no other students of color in the student body. Moreover, one notes that there was no mention of his interaction with his peers in his diary. Despite the pastoral venue of the seminary's location with the "rambling hills… in the suburbs of the village, and from their summits viewing the distant range of the Blue Mountains, and the sun setting gloriously over and behind them" which Payne certainly appreciated, still, he was far from home. This scene only intensified the homesickness which Payne experienced being away from his native state, South Carolina and "the low, prairie-like regions surrounding Charleston, where the sun seemed to rise out of the ocean and not set behind the islands.[93]

DEPARTURE

Although he enjoyed his theological studies, Payne's residency at Gettysburg Seminary came to an abrupt end. While reading, he experienced a sharp pain in the very eye which he damaged looking at a solar eclipse while preparing to teach his students in South Carolina. Again, the anguished and the tortured soul surfaces. The medical opinion was to rest his eyes and obtain prescription shaded lenses for his glasses. His life of a student was suddenly terminated. What course could he take now? What was left for him to do? To assist in sorting out these questions, Payne sought out President Schmucker for advice. This encounter marked a turning point in life's road for Payne and a decisive point American Church history. Payne inquired of Schmucker's assessment of his abilities and contributions to the church in light of this ailment. Payne noted Schmucker's response, "We should be glad to have you operate as a minister of the gospel in the Lutheran Church, but I think you can find a greater field of usefulness in the A.M.E. Church; therefore I advise you to join that body of professing Christians.[94] Always judicious and contemplative, Payne had to ponder and pray over such a decision and did not give Schmucker an immediate response. Lying on his bed, Payne was encouraged and stimulated by the words of St. Paul, "Woe to me if I preach not the gospel"(I Corinthians 9:16). It was at this point that Payne's vocational direction changed from the promising pedagogue to leadership in pastoral ministry.

Although the best construction placed on Schmucker's response would seem to indicate here that he was exercising that for which he was an advocate i.e., ecumenical spirit, his response also altered the rapprochement among African Americans and the Lutheran church on American soil. Apparently, Payne did not acknowledge any ambivalence or hesitancy on the part of Schmucker to continue to be the liberal churchman that was exhibited at the beginning of Payne's stay. Payne noted from the letter of recommendation that Schmucker gave to him:

> As you are about to leave the institution in which for about two years you have been pursuing a course of study preparatory to the holy ministry, it affords me unfeigned pleasure to testify that the effect of our daily intercourse during this time has been in unwavering confidence in the integrity of your purposes and the excellence of our character, together with the conviction that the God 'who one of one blood made all nations to dwell upon the face of the earth; will accompany you through life and crown with his blessing your labors in behalf of our oppressed kinsmen after the flesh.[95]

This letter is significant for two important reasons. First, it asserts that Payne had frequent encounters with Schmucker while a student. Second, it indicates that although Payne pursued theological education to better equip himself to be a better teacher, he had changed his vocational plans, now seeing himself called to the pastoral ministry. Apparently, Schmucker had noticed something in Payne that Payne had not seen in himself. While Payne embraced Lutheranism through confirmation, he was still a Methodist at heart. Payne described Schmucker's reaction to his decision by stating, "his advice [was] agreeable to my Methodistic predilections."[96] With the decision made and having already become acquainted with the A.M.E. Church from his work in Carlisle, Pennsylvania, Payne departed from Gettysburg for Philadelphia. Although Payne left without receiving the theological degree, he was not different from many of his colleagues. Many students never completed the full course of studies in theology. With letters of recommendations from Schmucker and Krauth, he reversed his travels from two years ago.

About these Gettysburg years Coan suggests that Payne's experience there helped him to be centered on the reality of God's power, goodness, and mercy; provided an opportunity for self-examination in light of the will of God, countered his feelings of unworthiness, wandering mind and impure thoughts with the desire to live the sanctified life; and enabled recurring acts of self-dedication. For Coan these are summed up in Payne's practice of private devotions while at Gettysburg. In addition, Coan feels that Gettysburg provided the environment which was the catalyst for Payne venturing into public ministry. Moreover, the seminary at Gettysburg provided him the wherewithal to make a valuable contribution to American Christianity. This writer would venture to say that Gettysburg's institutional leadership in Schmucker provided one of the model's of ecclesiastical leadership. Following his years at Gettysburg, Payne addressed correspondence to Schmucker as the "venerable preceptor." Schmucker also provided ecumenical leadership which Payne exhibited in his future life as Bishop in the AME Church.

This chapter has focused on the first twenty-six years of Daniel Payne's life. These were the formative years for the future ecclesiastical and educational leader the African Methodist Episcopal Church. The contributions of strong familial bonds with his mother, father, and aunt; good basic education at the Minor's Moralist School; self-education, mentors, religious education in the Methodist Sunday school; and quality theological studies at Gettysburg Lutheran Seminary were important for his professional development. These were also years of tension and transition for Payne: the move from the slaveholding state of South Carolina to the freedom of the North in New York and Pennsylvania; from baptism and formation in the Methodist Church to confirmation and theological education in the Lutheran Church; from founder and primary school educator of a successful school to banished pedagogue. Such tensions, and transitions, along with familial and community support systems, will be interwoven as Payne's life story continues to unfold.

NOTES

1. Daniel Alexander Payne, *Recollections of Seventy Years* (Nashville: Publishers House of the A.M.E. Sunday School Union, 1888). http://docsouth.unc.edu/church/payne70/menu.html.

2. Ibid., 11.

3. Ibid., 12.

4. Ibid., 13.

5. Ibid., 14; see also "Rules and Regulations of the Brown Fellowship" Society (Charleston, SC, 1 November 1790); see also Carter Woodson, *The Education of the Negro Prior to 1861* (Washington, D.C.: The Associated Publishers, 1919; reprint, Salem, New Hampshire: Ayer, 1991), 129.

6. *Recollections*, 15.

7. Caleb Bingham, *The Columbian Orator*, David W. Blight ed. (New York: New York University Press, 1998) reprint edition, 3.

8. Richard L. Johannesen, "Caleb Bingham's *American Preceptor* and *Columbian Orator*" *The Speech Teacher* (March 1969): 142.

9. Ibid., 142–143.

10. *Recollections*, 15.

11. Ibid., 15.

12. Rev. J. Brown Patterson, "Memoir of the Rev. John Brown," in *The Self-Interpreting Bible*, (Glasgow: Blackie, Fullerton, and Co., 1830), vi.

13. *Recollections*, 17.

14. Bernard Powers, *Black Charlestonians: A Social History*, 1822–1885 (Fayetteville: University of Arkansas Press, 1994), 2.

15. Ibid., 10; see also, Carter, 129.

16. Powers, 11.

17. Ibid., 3.

18. Ibid., 36.

19. Ibid., 38.

20. Ibid., 43.

21. Ibid., 40.

22. Ibid., 51.

23. Ibid., 54.

24. Ibid., 61.

25. Ibid., 62; see also John Hope Franklin and Alfred A. Moss, Jr. *From Slavery to Freedom*. New York: Alfred A. Knopf, 2006, 164–166.

26. *Recollections*, 20.

27. Ibid.

28. *Recollections*, 23.

29. Lindley Murray, *English Grammar Adapted to the Different Classes of Learners with An Appendix Containing Rules and Observations, For Assisting the More Advanced Students to Write with Perspicuity and Accuracy* (Philadelphia: Freeman Scott, 1877); *Recollections*, 21.

30. Murray, 3.

31. William F. Woods, "The Evolution of Nineteenth-Century Grammar Teaching," in *Rhetoric Review* 5 (Fall 1986): 6.

32. John Playfair, *Elements of Geometry Containing the First Six Books of Euclid, with a Supplement on the Quadrature of the circle, and the geometry of Solids: to Which are Added Elements of Plane and Spherical Trigonometry*, (New York: Collins and Hannay, 1833); see also *Recollections*, 22 and Ivor F. Goodson and Colin J. Marsh, *Studying School Subjects*, (London: The Palmer Press, 1996), 82–83.

33. Playfair, xvi.

34. Robert Zais, *Curriculum* (1976); This subject was directed to the practical use of the new machines and appliances which were being used. The inclusion of chemistry, astronomy, and botany were introduced into the American curriculum during the national period. They were incorporated for the practical implications of living in the nation; *Recollections*, 22.

35. Elijah Hinsdale Burritt, *The Geography of the Heavens or, Familiar Instruction for Finishing the Visible Stars and Constellations*, (Hartford: F.J. Huntington, 1833).The text includes topics such as "Description for Commencing the Study of the Star," "Origin of the Constellation," "Directions for Knowing the Planets. Each

lesson contained questions in order for the teachers to examine the students; *Recollections*, 22.

36. Ibid., iii.

37. Ibid.

38. *Recollections*, 22.

39. Ibid., 22–23.

40. Ibid., 24.

41. Raymond Morris Bost "The Reverend John Bachman and the Development of Southern Lutheranism." Ph.D. diss., Yale University, 1963, Summary.

42. *Recollections*, 24.

43. Ibid., 27; No. 2639 An Act to Amend the Law Relating to Slaves and Free Persons of Color, Be it enacted by the honorable, the Senate and House of Representatives, now met and sitting in General Assembly, and by the authority of the same: If any person shall hereafter teach any slave to read or write, or cause, or procure any slave to read or write, such person, if a free white person, upon conviction thereof shall for each and every offense against this Act be fined not exceeding one hundred dollars and imprisoned not more than six months; or, if a free person of color, shall be whipped not exceeding fifty lashes and fined not exceeding fifty dollars, at the discretion of the court of magistrates and freeholders before which such person of color is tried; and if a slave, to be whipped at the discretion of the court, not exceeding fifty lashes: the informer to be entitled to one-half of the fine, and to be a competent witness. And if any free person of color or slave shall keep any school or other place of instruction for teaching any slave or free person of color to read or write, such free person of color or slave shall be liable to the same fine, imprisonment, and corporal punishment as are by this Act imposed and inflicted on free persons of color and slaves for teaching slaves to read or write.

44. *Recollections*, 25.

45. Ibid., 28.

46. Ibid.

47. Ibid., 33.

48. Ibid., 34. The list included Drs. William Capers, Benjamin W. Palmer, John Bachman, Bishop Gadsen and Pastor Kennedy who was Payne's pastor. In addition, he mentions with high regard his visit to a Samuel Weston.

49. Ibid., 34.

50. Ibid., 36.

51. Ibid., 37.

52. Ibid., 41; Josephus Roosevelt Coan, *Daniel Alexander Payne Christian Educator*, (Philadelphia: The A.M.E. Book Concern, 1935), 20.

53. *Recollections*, 44.

54. Ibid., 44.

55. Ibid., 45.

56. *History of the Lutheran Church in South Carolina* (South Carolina Synod of the Lutheran Church in America, 1971), 904; *Proceedings of the Evangelical Lutheran Synod of S.Carolina and Adjacent States, Convened at St. Paul's Church, Newberry District, So.Ca., November, 1830*, (Charleston: James Burges, 1831), 10.

57. Abdel Ross Wentz, ed., *Gettysburg Theological Seminary* Alumni Record, vol. 2., (Harrisburg: Evangelical Press, 1964), 1835; see also, Daniel A. Payne, "Dedication" in *The Semi-Centenary and the Retrospection of the African Methodist Episcopal Church*, (Baltimore: Sharewood, 1866), reprint edition (Freeport, NY: Books for Libraries Press, 1967), n.p.

58. Coan, 20.

59. Constitution, Bye-laws of the Evangelical Lutheran Society on Missions and the Proceedings.

60. Minutes of the Proceedings of the Missionary Society of the Lutheran Theological Seminary, Gettysburg, Pennsylvania, 4 March 1835.

61. Samuel Simon Schmucker, *Elements of Popular Theology with Special Reference to the Doctrines of the Reformation, as Avowed before the Diet at Augsburg in MDXXX* (1st ed; Andover: Gould and Newman, 1834). This is popularly entitled, *Popular Theology*.

62. Ibid., 248.

63. Ibid., 252.

64. *Recollections*, 45.

65. Ibid., 48.

66. Ibid., 50.

67. Charles Kenmore Killian "Bishop Daniel A. Payne: Black Spokesman for Reform" (Dissertation: Indiana University, 1971), 77.

68. *Recollections*, 49.

69. *Recollections*, 51–55.

70. *Recollections*, 57.

71. Abdel Ross Wentz, *Pioneer in Christian Unity* (Philadelphia: Fortress Press, 1967) reprint edition (Gettysburg, PA: Lutheran Theological Seminary at Gettysburg), 146.

72. Ibid., 147.

73. William N Sholl, Gettysburg, to the Students of the Theological Seminary South Carolina, 29, June 1835, transcript in the hand of William N. Sholl, Archives, Wentz Library, Lutheran Theological Seminary at Gettysburg.

74. Minutes of the Proceedings of the Society for the Inquiry on Missions, 1 July 1835; 5 August 1835; 2 September 1835; 6 April 1836; 6 December 1836; 4 January 1837; 5 April 1837.

75. Minutes of the Proceedings of the Society of the Inquiry on Missions, 6 January 1836 where he reports on his visit to a mission point in Carlisle; 2 March 1836 where he reads a paper entitled, "On the Prospects (?) of the Church of Christ in Heathen Lands;"1 March 1837.

76. Ibid., 1 July 1835.

77. Ibid., 1 August 1836.

78. Diary 20 August 1835; September 1835; October 1835; 1 January 1836; 21 March 1836; 12 May 1836; 30 August 1836; 18 September 1836; 30 October 1836;15 October 1836; 23 October 1836; 8 November 1836 in Coan, 22–47.

79. Ibid., September 1835 in Coan, 27.

80. *Encyclopedia of Religion*, "Pietism;" see also Mark Noll, *A History of Christianity in the United States and Canada* (Grand Rapids: Eerdmans, 1992), 70–71; Paul P. Kuenning, *The Rise and Fall of American Lutheran Pietism* (Macon, Georgia: Mercer University Press, 1988).

81. Wentz, 134.

82. Samuel Simon Schmucker, *An Inaugural Address Delivered Before the Directors of the Theological Seminary of the General Synod of the Evangelical Lutheran Church* (Carlisle, PA: J. Tizzard and J. Crover, 1826).

83. *Catalogue of the Officers and Students of the Theological Seminary of the General Synod of the Lutheran Church Located at Gettysburg, PA. September 1827.*

84. Schmucker, *An Inaugural Address*, 28–30.

85. Minutes of the Proceedings of the Lutheran Society of Inquiry on Missions, 1 April 1835.

86. Schmucker, *An Inaugural Address*, 24.

87. Diary, October 1835.

88. Coan, 30.

89. *Recollections*, 61.

90. Coan, 35.

91. *The Republican Compiler,* 20 December 1836.

92. Coan, 38, 46, 47.

93. *Recollections*, 57.

94. Ibid., 61.

95. Ibid., 62.

96. Ibid.

Chapter Two

The Transition Years: 1837–1856

With the termination of his theological studies at Gettysburg Seminary, Payne had to muster once again the energy to discern and explore his options for his life's work. Although living within the Lutheran faith community, Payne's individual world-view continues to expand. At times the expanding world-view drove him into situations beyond his control, but at other times, Payne clearly makes decisions based on his experience and sense of call by God. This chapter examines and chronicles several levels of transition: Payne's move from being the licensed layman to being ordained and added to the roster of the Lutheran Church; from the roster of the Lutheran Church to the roster of the African Methodist Episcopal Church; from parish pastor to esteemed Bishop. While education continues to be a vital force in this period, one also sees his life in the context of the growth and development of the African Methodist Episcopal Church.

THE LUTHERAN CLERGYMAN

The year of 1837 was a fortuitous one for Payne despite the medical setback and the disappointment of not finishing his formal theological studies. Payne returned to Philadelphia to consult with Bishop Morris Brown of the African Methodist Episcopal Church. Bishop Brown, like Payne, was a native of Charleston, South Carolina. Brown was admitted to full connection with the AME Church in 1818 at the General Conference.[1] Ten years later, the General Conference held in Philadelphia, elected and consecrated Morris Brown bishop, 25 May 1828. While not lettered or formally educated, Payne felt that he made an impression on those who heard him.[2] More importantly, especially as a strong advocate of education, Payne described his side of Brown with the following words:

> We, and all who knew him, can truthfully say, that notwithstanding all the liter-
> ary disadvantages under which he labored, he was, in spirit, abreast of the age,
> and to the utmost of his knowledge and power encouraged the education of his
> people. We can furnish no greater evidence of this than where he is seen refus-
> ing to ordain a young itinerant because he had not the literary qualifications
> required by the Discipline.[3]

Payne intended to affiliate with that denomination, however, through cor-respondence with a friend of his late father, Payne learned that much of the denomination's clergy leadership opposed the idea of educated clergy. This attitude was supported by such avowals by AME ministers as "we never studied Latin or Greek" or "never studied Hebrew" or "not rubbed their heads against college walls."[4] With his life to date committed to education for himself as well as others, Payne was not interested in fighting the education battle and he opted to connect with a new Lutheran body, for the spring of 1837 was also the time of the formation of the Franckean Synod. This synod was created and established to be a direct confrontation with the Hartwick Synod in their failure to speak out against the institution of slavery. Taking the name of Franckean to reflect the respect and regard they had for August Herman Francke, the German pietist, the synod thus combined two elements of Payne's vocation: piety and abolition. It isn't difficult to imagine Payne embracing his brothers in this newly established synod with its abolitionist stance.[5]

The first meeting of the Franckean Synod took place on 24 May 1837 in Fordsbush, New York. The synod's constitution underscored its commit-ment to the anti-slavery movement through the makeup of the delegates. In describing the delegates who were permitted to attend, it stated, "No person shall be entitled to a seat in this Synod as delegate who has not attained the age of twenty-one years, and who is not a regular communicant member of the church. Neither shall he be a slaveholder, nor engaged directly or indirectly in the manufacture and traffic of intoxicating liquors to be used as a beverage."[6]

Payne was admitted to the Synod as a licentiate in June of that year. As a licentiate one was able to take on ministerial functions as approved by the Conference to which the candidate belonged, visit churches and pursue theological education in a program of studies that was recommended by the Synod.[7] The qualifications and demonstration of true piety and real conver-sion to God were validated by membership in a congregation. In an address at the inaugural meeting of the Synod, John D. Lawyer the president of the Synod, underscored the importance given to piety when he stated,

> I would take the liberty to inquire whether applicants for the ministerial office are examined with sufficient closeness and rigor, on the subject of their own conversion. If they lack personal piety, they will be blind leaders of the blind. It is much better to have only a few ministers of the right sort, than many of the wrong kind....Though I am no despiser, of colleges and of college-learning, yet I think learning is not the only, and not even the chief thing for a minister. A plain taught minister with plain common sense, and a heart full of love to God and perishing sinners, is worth a dozen of the former description, who are not converted. The oversight in admitting men into the ministry whose hearts are not right with God, is the most deplorable of all errors that a church can commit.[8]

He goes on to describe the criteria that he might use for the licentiate with the following:

> My opinion is, therefore, that every good man of sound sense, who has a desire and a capacity for extended usefulness in the church should be hunted up by the ministers, and be encouraged in the way I stated....Such men would not be qualified to take charge of churches. Such men would not be the most learned, but they would certainly not be the least useful class of ministers. They would have experience before they entered the ministry; they would be well-tried men, and men of serious habits, of solid sense, of tact and skill in winning souls to the side of religion.[9]

Payne must have demonstrated his level of religious piety and devotion for he was approved as a licensed preacher on May 31, 1837 following the close of the meeting. Payne noted that immediately following his approval he began to serve as pastor of the Liberty Street Presbyterian Church in East Troy, New York because there was no call or assignment for him in the Lutheran Church.[10] He also mentioned that he was considered by two other congregations in two different denominations, one, a congregation of the Presbyterian Church and the other, a congregation of the Protestant Episcopal Church.[11] With a letter of permission to serve the Troy congregation from the President of the Franckean Synod, Payne began his pastoral work. The Synodical President in addressing the action the following year stated that Payne had demonstrated his personal piety, qualifications, and good references from faculty members and Lutheran pastors.[12] Payne was listed in the *Minutes of the Meeting* the following year as a delegate from Troy, New York. However, Payne was not in attendance, but sent a report of his activities. He stated the reason for this absence was due to illness. His report indicated his continued growth in piety and pastoral leadership. It also outlined the scope of his ministry in upstate New York as he wrote the following:

> I have under my pastoral care 47 church members. Congregation varies from 150 to 200. State of Piety. During the first part of the winter past, the tone of religious feelings was very deep. There was a general cry for pure hearts and the conversion of sinners.[13]

He described a fugitive salve woman who was admitted into the membership of the congregation which certainly caused some anxiety on the part of the congregants. He went on to say, "Just as the work above mentions was in progress and many were awakened to a sense of the danger, it pleased the Lord to afflict me with a very severe sore throat, and as I had no one to follow up my labors, it ceased."[14]

Payne's report also included the growth and vibrancy of the year-long Sunday School which flourished throughout the year, with approximately one-third of the students being people of color. It also encompassed a broad age-span with students from four years to sixty years of age. In addition, there were several groups or societies dedicated to outreach: Foreign Missions, Temperance, Benevolence for females and the Sunday School Assistant Society.[15] This report suggested a vibrant congregational life under his leadership, remarkable considering that Payne at twenty-six, had had no previous pastoral experience.

The quality and strength of Payne's leadership was immediately noticed by others in the Troy community. Although he was steeped in the life of the parish pastor, he was asked to represent his community at a meeting of the National Moral Reform Society which was meeting in Philadelphia, Pennsylvania from the fourteenth through nineteenth of August 1837.[16] The society was developed by Blacks to describe, condemn, and abolish the institution of slavery in the United States. The opening declaration at this inaugural meeting states the following:

> We rejoice that we are thrown into a revolution where the contest is not for landed territory, but for freedom; the weapons not carnal, but spiritual; where struggle is not for blood, but for right; and where the bow is the power of God, and the arrow the instrument of divine justice; while the victims are the devices of reason, and the prejudice of the human heart. It is in this glorious struggle for civil and religious liberty, for the establishment of peace on earth and good will to men, that we morally bound by all the relative ties we owe to the author of our being, to enter the arena and boldly contend for victory. Our reliance and only hope is in God.[17]

The founders also sought to be a voice and movement that countered the American Colonization Society whose focus centered on the return of Blacks to the African continent. They also opposed the American Anti-Slavery Society which they saw as not adamant enough about the injustice of slavery. The Moral Society therefore stated,

> We therefore declare to the world, that our subject is to extend the principles
> of universal peace and good will to all mankind, by promoting sound morality,
> by the influence of education, temperance, economy, and all those virtues that
> alone can render man acceptable in the eyes of God or the civilized world.[18]

Education, Temperance, Economy, and Universal Liberty were the overarching themes of the organization. These themes certainly were of interest to Payne played an active role in the formation of the Society through his participation in the work as a committee member as well as spiritual contributor.[19] But again, education was integral to the Society's work and objectives, and Payne would certainly have agreed with the statements of James Forten, Jr. who addressed the society and emphasized the importance of education on the second to last day of the meetings:

> One of the many things held out by the Society for our benefit, there is none
> stands more prominent than Education; and it is to this subject that I shall chiefly
> confine my remarks. Sir, the best feelings of our nature, our highest aspirations
> should be directed towards the illumination of the mind. It is a prize far above
> all others, and so great is its influence, so irresistible and captivating is its form,
> that should it come in the glittering mantle of courtly dignity, or in the tattered
> grab of beggary, or shine beneath the dark colouring of our skin, its potency
> must be felt and known; proscription cannot live where it lives; the oppressor
> must with under it, and be compelled to lift his murderous foot from off the
> neck of the oppressed. Education molds the character; it is the food of morality;
> nourishing the mental faculties, checking the tide of vice, subduing the violent
> passions and natural depravity which pervade the human breast, it renders man
> an ornament to society, a beautiful, intellectual and virtuous being; it gives him
> to know fully his relation to the Deity, inspires him with a dignity, possesses
> him with a commanding mien, of which no power on earth can disrobe him.
> Sir, as an evidence that these are some of the wholesome effects produced from
> cultivating and enriching the mind, we have only to take a retrospective view of
> things, to glance our eyes over the innumerable pages of history.

He goes on to say,

> Hence where Education predominates, there no enemy can intrude to spoil or
> contaminate domestic happiness. That Education is conductive to economy, no
> one will for a moment question.

Knowledge is power; and in proportion to the acquirement of it, when fitly and aptly applied, is the progress of morality,—discord and strife are laid prostrate, and peace asserts its empire, vice and immorality are immolated, and virtue and reform live to confine, quality, and regulate the emotions of the heart. Education cannot help but improve the morals; for it and morality go hand in hand; they are in many respects dependent upon each other; in fact, they are almost diametrically joined. It is far beyond all calculation how much we owe to their power for the little quiet we now enjoy; and without these great essentials to man's what kind of a world would we have?[20]

Payne encountered a number of the leading anti-slavery spokespersons and activists as the meeting. Among those were the Rev. Samuel E. Cornish[21] who was editor of the *Colored American* and Joshua Leavitt, of the *New York Evangelist*.[22] On his return home he lodged at the home of a Mrs. Asenath Nicholson Graham where he met Theodore Weld who asked him to preach in Shiloh Presbyterian Church[23] and Lewis Tappen who was on the executive board of the Anti-Slavery Society.[24] There can be no doubt that Payne discussed the issues of slavery with these leaders in the boarding house, for no sooner had he returned to Troy, New York, than he received an invitation to be part of the speaking circuit for the Anti-Slavery Society. Although it was a flattering offer, Payne had another difficult decision to make with an offer of an annual salary of $300 and travel expenses to entice the young pastor. He sought counsel for discerning his decision. After all, how could he renege on his divine calling to the pastorate? Payne responded succinctly when he wrote, "But I had consecrated myself to the pulpit and the work of salvation. Could I turn aside from so high a position and so holy a calling?"[25] To this end, he discussed the issue with Lawyer Yates who shared with Payne the fact that he himself had changed careers through the advice of others but he now regretted the decisions. Yates added, "I think God has called you to the pulpit, and therefore advise that you stick to theology and the work of the Christian ministry."[26] Payne's deliberations and discernment resulted in the following correspondence:

Troy, (N.Y.) Sept. 18, 1837
Rev. and Dear Sir,
I received your epistle dated Sept. 11th, on the 14th, and was made happy with the spirit that it breathes, as well as with the information it contains. You say that "the Executive Committee instructed" you to "invite" me "to be present on that occasion," to assist us by public address. I am deeply sensible of the great honor which such an invitation confers upon me, and fell truly humbled beneath it. You will please inform the Committee that they have my unfeigned thanks for his token of their high esteem. Assure them that nothing but an insurmountable obstacle prevents my compliance with their request—and that while I make this statement, I feel regret, bordering upon anguish.

Would to heaven it were otherwise!—and that I could appear in your midst to plead the cause of my afflicted people! I have reason to do it. I have been in their smoky huts on Southern plantations, where degradation and misery reign! I have seen the aged mother robbed of her children; marked the streams of sorrow which rolled down her furrowed cheek—and heard the deep sign of her broken heart, as she lifted her imploring eyes to Heaven for that succor which she could not obtain on earth!

I have seen the anguished husband and his weeping wife separated, never to see each other until they met in the world of the spirits! I have seen men and women—beings upon whose souls the impress of the Deity was stamped—born to inherit the heavens—destined to tune the harps of glory before the throne of the Eternal, bound in chains and driven to the Orleans market like so many beasts! Shall I proceed? O, sir!—Reverend brother, my heart is pained within me! My soul is sick! My hand trembles as I think upon the abominations of slavery which my eyes have beheld! Sir, I am opposed to slavery because it wars against earth and Heaven!

It wars against earth—it robs man of his inalienable rights—tramples his tenderest relations under feet—gives his social and connubial comforts to the sighing winds, and envelops his deathless spirit in the black clouds of ignorance!

It wars against heaven. With the audacity of Lucifer, he approaches the temples of the living God, driving men from its altars, binding and casting them into prison; it seals the book of life, and gags the ministers of Christ!

This sin is the legitimate operation of its code. A code which none but tyrants sanction—which militates against the Declaration of Independence, disgraces our country, and makes it the scorn of nations—the pity of angels—and the glory of fiends!

Heaven be praised for the existence of the American Anti-Slavery Society, (of which yours is a branch.) I consider it the mediator between a guilty nation and the indignant Ruler of the Universe. It has created a ban of philanthropists, whose principles are not the offspring of fanatical brains; mother of wise philosophers, nor yet of pious and learned doctors of divinity.—No, sir; their principles are older than the foundations of the earth!—They were, when "the morning stars sang together, and all the sons of God shouted for joy." Then, sir, when newborn earth hung verdant in the smiling heaven, did the great, impartial Jehovah give to his youngest, last-created son, Adam, those principles to be transmitted to his progeny, as their inalienable, eternal inheritance.

Apostles of holy freedom, onward, onward, onward!—for your success my tears shall fall—my signs, my groans, my prayers, ascend in the presence of HIM who commanded you to plead the cause of the oppressed!

With profound respect, I am yours
In the cause of holy freedom,

DANIEL A. PAYNE[27]

Payne's difficult decision not to embark on the anti-slavery circuit brought him to the fork in the road and a major life decision that had to be made. Payne gives us a glimpse of his decision-making process by indicating his awareness of individual God-given gifts or talents of all people. He reflected on the work of Frederick Douglass, the African American abolitionist and one of the foremost, if not the most celebrated orators of the nineteenth century. Payne stated, "Frederick Douglass was fitted for his specialty; Daniel A. Payne for his."[28] His reservations centered on the issue of vocation. These reflections also suggest that he pondered the question in light of the scriptures. In particular, one cannot help think of Paul's first letter to the Corinthians in Chapter 12 where he discerns the gift of the Spirit.

[4]Now there are diversities of gifts, but the same Spirit.
[5]And there are differences of administrations, but the same Lord.
[6]And there are diversities of operations, but it is the same God which worketh all in all.
[7]But the manifestation of the Spirit is given to every man to profit withal.
[8]For to one is given by the Spirit the word of wisdom; to another the word of knowledge by the same Spirit;
[9]To another faith by the same Spirit; to another the gifts of healing by the same Spirit;
[10]To another the working of miracles; to another prophecy; to another discerning of spirits; to another divers kinds of tongues; to another the interpretation of tongues:
[11]But all these worketh that one and the selfsame Spirit, dividing to every man severally as he will. (KJV)

In Payne's discernment, to go against God's call for his life might bring him ruin. This decision was timely in that on New Year's Eve 1837 while preaching, he lost his voice.

During this time of convalescence, Gerrit Smith, whom Payne regards as "the great philanthropist" and "champion of human freedom"[29] visited Payne. Smith, a member of the Presbyterian Church, supported the temperance effort, The American Bible Society, and the American Sunday School Union. Initially, he had been an advocate of the relocating of Blacks back to Africa, but eventually supported immediate emancipation and their full participation in American society. Smith later supported, financially, the efforts of John Brown at Harper's Ferry. He was also a strong supporter of women's rights.[30]

His philanthropy extended to the economic well-being of Blacks, as he designated land for poor Blacks to cultivate in order for them to be economically
independent. He remained an ardent spokesperson for the equality of all.

Payne returned the visit of Smith by visiting his home in Petersboro, New
York where he stayed for four days. While there, he also visited the Oneida
Institute and spoke with President Green. Established in 1827, the Oneida Institute in Whitesboro, New York began as a school to educate students for the
mission field in the Western United States. Beriah Green became president of
the school in 1833. Educated at Andover Newton, he was a staunch opponent
of the American Colonization Society. As Milton Sernett wrote,

> Green accepted the presidency in 1833 under to conditions. He must be free to
> preach immediatism. He was also allowed to admit student regardless of race.
> This last and equally import objective was, in the final analysis much more
> radical than remodeling the Institute into an abolitionist institution. Green envi-
> sioned his school as a model biracial and prejudice-free community.[31]

Without the assurance of regaining the use of his voice in the immediate future, Payne resigned as pastor of the congregation and returned to Carlisle in
south central Pennsylvania to continue his recuperation.

On 6 June 1839 the Franckean Synod held its annual meeting. Payne, as a
candidate for ordination, stood before the Committee on Examination from
3 to 8 PM and before the Ministerium. In an open forum, Payne along with
others was examined in Hebrew and Greek. Upon completion of the examination, Payne along with a Henry Dox was elected to the office of Bishop.[32]
Three days later 9 June, Payne's ordination took place at 10:00 AM with
the secretary of the Synod preaching on the text 2 Timothy 4:2: "Preach the
word; be instant in season, out of season; reprove, rebuke, exhort with all
longsuffering and doctrine." (KJV)

On the same evening, at 7:30 PM at the last session, the synod met in worship, where the emphasis for the evening was on Missions. It was Payne's
time to preach. He used 1 Corinthians 16:22, "if any man love not the Lord
Jesus Christ, let him be Anathema, Maranatha" as the text for the sermon. In
it, Payne spoke in support of the resolution before the Synod from the Committee on American Slavery. He begins with a large view of the offense of
slavery:

> I am opposed to slavery, not because it enslaves the black man, but because it
> enslaves man. And were all the slave-holders in this land men of color, and the
> slaves white men, I would be a through and uncompromising an abolitionist
> as I now am; for where and whenever I may see a being in the form of a man,
> enslaved by his fellow man, without respect to his complexion, I shall life up my
> voice to plead his cause, against all claims of his proud oppressor; and I shall

do it not merely from the sympathy which man feels towards suffering man, but because of God, the living God, whom I dare not disobey, has commanded me to open my mouth for the dumb, and to plead the cause of the oppressed.[33]

Payne went on to describe the conditions and living of slaves that he had observed with his own eyes and heard with his ears from the slaves themselves. Even the preaching of the Gospel was forbidden by the slave-masters. This goes against the law of God, or in Payne's words, "it subverts the moral government of God." Although some might say that there are missions in the Methodist and Lutheran churches in the southern States and that slave-masters are open to exposing the slave to the message of the Gospel, however, this does not negate the fact that this is against the law of God. He concludes with the call to freedom, "O Brethren of the Franckean Synod! Awake! To the battle, and hurl the hottest thunders of divine truth at the head of this cruel monster, until he shall fall to rise no more; and the groans of the enslaved are converted into the songs of the free!"[34]

Payne, upon gaining use of voice, devoted himself to general education and later went to Philadelphia which had a large Black population. Although he didn't feel able to take on the proclamation of the Word through preaching, he could not sit idle. He decided to return to the teaching field and in 1840 he opened a grammar school in June. Payne was not the first to establish a school for Black students in the city, however, the other two schools had closed within a year, and those students came to the school established by Payne. Already immersed in a school, Payne developed and encouraged the work of a theological association which assisted in the cultivation of biblical knowledge and the respective sciences. In addition, he established a literary society and Sunday School. These years continue to be marked by Payne's efforts at negotiating the shifting circumstances and contexts of his calling.

ENCOUNTER AND CONNECTION
WITH THE A.M.E. CHURCH

It was during this time period that he became reacquainted with the clergy of the African Methodist Episcopal Church. In particular, he mentioned Bishop Morris Brown, Dr. Bias of Bethel AME Church, and the Rev. Richard Robinson. With these encounters he found a growing attraction to the denomination. One might say he felt "called" to that denomination. When Payne reflected on this part of his life he felt that it was his duty to become affiliated with the denomination. Apparently, he also corresponded with this Lutheran mentor, President Schmucker, about his decision to change denominations, for he wrote, "Then my venerable preceptor, Dr. Schmucker, also still advised me to

enter this branch of the Christian Church"[35] One recalls four years previously
that it was Schmucker who suggested that Payne affiliate with the African
Methodist Episcopal Church upon leaving Gettysburg Seminary. Payne continued to be in contact with his Lutheran mentor. In a piece of correspondence
Payne wrote about his work in Philadelphia:

> Philadelphia, March 20, 1841
> My Ever Venerable Preceptor.
> You will perceive from this circular what I am doing in the City of P. I did not
> succeed in obtaining an appointment as a city missionary it being beyond the
> province of the Society to which you referred me to make such an appointment
> though I was received with great affection by Pas. Wm. Barnes. I opened this
> Seminary the 15 of last June under considerable disadvantage of a local char-
> acter. It has been gradually increasing ever since and now number 23 pupils of
> both sexes, varying in ages from 6 to 18 years. The greatest numbers are now
> in the second [classes] studying grammar. Three are in the third class studying
> geometry and any advice on instruction calculated to improve my seminary
> either on morals or science will be gratefully received.
> Yours affectionately
> D.A. Payne
> P.S. Please sir tender my sincere regard to Dr. Krauth and also to any of the
> student who may know me.[36]

It was during the winter of 1841 that Payne joined the Quarterly Conference
at Bethel Church in Philadelphia. At the same time Bishop Morris Brown appointed to be superintendent. In this role, Payne had responsibility to making
sure there was a preacher for the services at Bethel. This afforded him the opportunity to listen to the preaching services rather than have that responsibility.
He listened to the proclamation, and as a theologically trained mind, was able
to exegete and reflect on the sermons as well as listen for delivery, content,
and organization. Upon his return to his home, he wrote his assessment of the
sermon.[37] One is reminded of Martin Luther, the sixteenth century reformer
who ventured into churches and commented on what he heard in which we
have a glimpse of his thoughts in the Preface to his *Small Catechism*. Payne's
comments consisted of such statements as "Brother Tillman…needs to know
the meaning of words…Brother Wilkerson is an intelligent preacher…Brother
Baker preached in his usual vague and indefinite manner.[38]

   On 21 May 1842, at the Philadelphia Conference, Payne was accepted as
a preacher of the church on a trial basis.[39] At the District meeting that Payne
brought the issue of education before the representatives. This included a
resolution for the education of the elders, deacons, and licensed preachers. He
further recommended a course of study "for our excellent discipline cannot
be fully executed; nor our present plan of improvement fully consummated

without an intelligent ministry."[40] One year later, 20 May 1843, Payne was admitted into full connection and to the itinerant ministry soon afterwards.[41] He was connected to the annual conference and subject to travel to various preaching assignments by the bishop. At his District Conference, Payne also presented a proposal on ministerial education for consideration by the General Conference which continued to be discussed and debated to the end of that year. What brought him to this denomination after his strong opposition to affiliating with them four years previous to this step? Perhaps a partial response to this question might be the very nature of the AME Church in regards to the Black population at that time and its formation as a denomination in the previous century.

The beginning of the AME Church is rooted in Philadelphia, Pennsylvania and the ministry of Richard Allen within the Methodist Episcopal Church. In the midst of a nation plagued by the bondage of Black women, men and children, "Richard Allen created an organization which gave liberty to all the Negro population who desired to worship at a shrine where no differences were made between bond and free, where there was no loss of self-respect by reason of the accident of color, and where the opportunity for service according to one's capacities was open to all.[42]

Richard Allen was born into slavery on February 14, 1760 in Philadelphia where he was raised as well as in Dover, Delaware.[43] His initial years were spent within the Quaker denomination. The Quakers were instrumental in giving religious instruction to the slaves for their conversion. Although some owned slaves they were advised to treat them well. In 1775 the state had the first Abolition Society organized and in 1780 it was the first state to pass a gradual emancipation act (Gradual Abolition Act) with the result of a developing a large free black citizenry. While in Dover, Delaware on the plantation of his master at about twenty years of age, he experienced a conversion and joined the Methodist denomination. In his autobiography he describes it:

> My sins were a heavy burden. I was tempted to believe there was no mercy for me. I cried to the Lord both night and day. One night I thought hell would be my portion. I cried unto Him who delighteth to hear the prayers of a poor sinner; and all of a sudden my dungeon shook, my chains flew off, and glory to God, I cried. My soul was filled. I cried, enough for me—the Saviour died. Now my confidence was strengthened that the Lord, for Christ's sake, and had heard my prayers, and pardoned all my sins. I was constrained to go from house to house, exhorting my old companions, and telling to all around what a dear Saviour I had found. I joined the Methodist society.[44]

Allen and his brother went the Methodist meetings and after a while his master and his wife allowed the preacher to come into their house. After several months the master was so moved that he allowed Richard and his brother to buy their freedom for two thousand dollars. Working at cutting wood, he eventually became an itinerate preacher traveling to East Jersey, Wilmington, Delaware, and eventually came to Pennsylvania in 1784 where he ventured to Lancaster, Little York, and then into Maryland.[45]

In December 1784 Allen attended the first meeting of the Methodist General Conference to be held in the United States, which was held in Baltimore, Maryland. The following year, Bishop Asbury asked Allen to travel with him. Asbury also directed him not to mix with the slaves when they would travel into the southern states and that he would have to sleep in the Bishop's carriage very often. Being a proud man, Allen stated he would not travel under those conditions. In addition, while he [Asbury] might be able to get help in case of emergency, that would not be the case for him. While Asbury asked him to think about the proposition, Allen traveled in Pennsylvania without support from the connection. When in need he would take employment to raise enough money to carry on. In his own words, "…I had many trials to pass through, and I received nothing from the Methodist connexion[sic]. My usual method was, when I would get bare of clothes, to stop travelling and go to work, so that no man could say I was chargeable to the connexion [sic]. My hands administered to my necessities."[46]

In February 1786, Allen returned to Philadelphia at the request of the elder. He was allowed to preach at the 5 AM service at St. George's Church, but there were times when he preached four or five times a day. He saw the important need of proclaiming the gospel to his enslaved brothers and sisters who, he felt, were neglected and not attending worship.

In the same year he began a society where people of color could worship. But when he proposed it to the Black elite, he met opposition. In spite of that he and three others organized prayer meetings and meetings of exhortation which were met with criticism from the elder who forbade it. Allen observed that this was directed to his colored brothers and sisters. It was interesting that the people who attended were members of St. George Church. The division between the white hierarchy and the members of color who continued to increase in the congregation came to a sharp turn in the road one Sunday morning. At first Blacks were relegated to the walls around the sanctuary; later, there was another dramatic turn of events. When Allen and others were entering the church to take their places, they were met by the sexton and told to go to the gallery. Determined to worship in the usual fashion, Allen recounts the following:

> …and on Sabbath morning we went to church and the sexton stood at the door, and told us to go in the gallery. He told us to go, and we would see where to sit. We expected to take the seats over the ones we formerly occupied below,

not knowing any better. We took those seats. Meeting had begun, and they were nearly done singing, and just as we got to the seats, the elder said, "let us pray." We had not been long upon our knees before I heard considerable scuffling and low talking. I raised my head up and saw one of the trustees, H—M—, having hold of the Rev. Absalom Jones, pulling him up off of his knees, and saying, "You must get up—you must not kneel here." Mr. Jones replied, "wait until prayer is over." Mr. H—M— said "no, you must get up now, or I will call for aid and I force you away." Mr. Jones said, "wait until prayer is over, and I will get up and trouble you no more." With that he beckoned to one of the other trustees, Mr. L—S— to come to his assistance. He came, and went to William White to pull him up. By this time prayer was over, and we all went out of the church in a body, and they were no more plagued with us in the church. This raised a great excitement and inquiry among the citizens, in so much that I believe they were ashamed of their conduct. But my dear Lord was with us, and we were filled with fresh vigour to get a house erected to worship God in. Seeing our forlorn and distressed situation, many of the hearts of our citizens were moved to urge us forward...[47]

That request on the part of the Elder became the fuel for the establishment of something different, a fellowship where one's skin color was not the criteria for participation. They initially found a room to rent for worship, however, John McClaskey of St. George Church, stated that they should cease raising funds or he would see to it that they were turned out of the meeting. He found no connection with their removal from the pews in St. George Church and their desire to be an independent worshipping community. He placed threats of expulsion. Allen wrote,

He told us that he wished us well, and that he was a friend to us, and used many arguments to convince us that we were wrong in building a church. We told him we had no place of worship; and we did not mean to go to St. George's church any more, as we were so scandalously treated in the presence of all the congregation present; "and if you deny us your name, you cannot seal up the scriptures from us, and deny us a name in heaven. We believe heaven is free for all who worship in spirit and truth." And he said, "so you are determined to go on." We told him—"yes, God being hour helper."[48]

A location was found by a committee but the antagonism from the Methodist connection continued. The Allen-Jones group broke ground and established the first African Church on American soil. The issue of denominational affiliation had to be decided. Allen and Jones wanted to be Methodist, the majority Church of England. The majority side prevailed. A committee from the African church wanted Allen as their pastor but he declined. He was committed to the Methodist tradition even with the racism he experienced. This commitment was based on the fact that the Methodist church was one of the first to reach out with the gospel to Blacks. As the same time he felt that the homiletical attraction of the denomination, that is, their preaching style was designed from the heart and extemporaneously delivered, not as a lecture. He felt that the doctrine was comprehensible to the people.[49] In Allen's own words, "...I told them I could not accept their offer, as I was a Methodist. I was indebted to the Methodists, under God, for what little religion I had; being convinced that they were the people of God, I informed them that I could not be any thing else but a Methodist, as I was born and awakened under them..."[50]

Allen purchased an old frame building and erected it on the land that was formerly of the Church of England, and in July 1794 Bishop Asbury preached at the first service of the church, Bethel. The interference from the Methodist Conference occurred again when it was suggested that the church be turned over to the Conference. An underhanded deal occurred when the members agreed to have the papers for incorporation drawn up; it was drawn up with incorporation into the Conference...the white Conference. This lasted ten years. Throughout the period the hierarchy wanted to dictate the preachers for the congregation, even to the point of legal action on the part of the Conference. But the courts ruled in favor of the society that the property was indeed theirs.

Thus in April 1816, a general meeting was held and a Conference was formed. The delegates approved the following resolution: "That the people of Philadelphia, Baltimore, &c.&c., should become one body, under the name of the African Methodist Episcopal Church."[51]

This background pushed Payne to affiliate with the denomination. This church body was fiercely proud of their cultural heritage and needs, committed to the gospel, and ready to assert their independence. It is striking, too, that the development of the denomination develops as the United States is asserting itself as an independent nation. It was just one year after the end of the War that began in 1812 and ended in 1815 with the Treaty of Ghent. Through battles with the English, the United States asserted its sovereignty against a world power. In this historic moment, the actions of the new church resonate more powerfully. With the approval of the resolution, the delegates of the now African Methodist Church asserted their identity as free people of God and beholden to none other. The also made a statement about their rootedness on American soil; they were part of these United States as well.

With the establishment of the church, members had to vote on ecclesiastical leadership and nomination and election of a Bishop. Although Richard Allen was one of the favorites in Payne's recording of the event, Daniel Coker was the Bishop-elect on April 9th; but by the very next day, he declined the office and Richard Allen was consecrated Bishop on April 11, 1816. It was the task of the Bishop to take responsibility for particular regions of the church. Allen did that, and at the same time, served as pastor of Bethel AME Church. Eventually, a council of Bishops was developed with supervisory responsibilities for the entire church. Payne captured that moment in the history of the church as well as the unique development in the lives of these men gathered in the conference he wrote, "Poor and lowly, an outcast and despised of men, it thus feebly entered into being; but with a manifest destiny of greatness which has been unmistakably developing for over three quarters of a century."[52] Bishop Allen exemplified these words when Payne recorded the witness of a Pastor Walter Proctor who wrote that the "house of Bishop Allen was a refuge for the oppressed and a house of the refugee from American oppression."[53] In addition, Allen was concerned with their spiritual and theological growth as well as their economic welfare. They were integrally related in Allen's eyes. Again, Payne noted, "Thoroughly 'anti-slavery,' his house was never shut 'against the friendless, homeless, penniless fugitives from the 'House of Bondage.'"[54]

Unfortunately, Payne was not privy to the words that were said or the speeches delivered during these momentous events. His recording of these events emerged from the oral interviews which he conducted. The first documentary evidence of the new church was recorded by Bishop Allen's son who at the age of fifteen was secretary for the Conference of 1818. It is safe to say that Payne's affiliation and subsequent membership in the AME Church was integrally combined with his commitment and identity with his brothers and sisters of color. Allen's commitment to his people would also have had an influence on Payne's sensitivity to the plight of his race.

Although Payne was admitted into full connection with the AME Church, he was still listed on the directory of the Franckean Synod of the Lutheran Church. In a memo addressed to the Synod in June of 1842, he asked to be removed immediately from the rolls of the Synod, informing the Synod that he connected with the "Colored Methodist Church." Although he owed a debt to the Synod, he stated that he was not able to cancel the debt at that time but that he would try by all means to do so. If he was not able to sever his ties with the Franckean Synod at that time, he requested that he be permitted to work with the church in "the principle of Christian Union" until his debt was paid and then he be dismissed. The committee recommended that Payne continue his association with the Synod until the debt was paid and then be released.[55]

Upon full connection with the AME Church in May 1843, Payne was called as an itinerant pastor to Israel Church in Washington, D.C. With this call by Bishop Brown, Payne was to serve for a minimum of one year. Accepting this call also meant that he would have to relinquish the school he had organized in Philadelphia to the Rev. Alexander Crummel who was at that time a deacon and missionary of the Protestant Episcopal church. Crummel was a formidable individual known as an avid nationalist, abolitionist and missionary. His family members were affiliated with the Protestant Episcopal Church. He attended the African Free School until his adolescent years and then went to the Noyes Academy in Canaan, New Hampshire, however, he had to complete his studies at Oneida Institute in Whitesboro, New York due to mob violence against Black students at Canaan. Encouraged by his home pastor to study toward ordination, Crummel applied to General Theological Seminary in New York City but he was rejected. Notwithstanding the rejection, Crummel attended lectures at Yale University and studied privately with clergymen in the New England area. He was ordained an Episcopal priest in 1842 and was called small congregations in Philadelphia and New York. It was during this period in time that he and Payne became acquainted.

Examining his life further, one can see the rapport that Crummel and Payne developed. Crummel was an intellectual. He went to England in 1848 with the primary purpose of raising funds for his parish, however, he prepared with tutor and entered Cambridge University where he received his Bachelor of Arts degree in 1853. From 1853 through 1872 he lived in Liberia returning to the States only twice to raise funds. He established St. Luke's Episcopal Church in Washington, DC in 1879 where he tended the congregation until 1894 upon his retirement. Although he was a strong anglophile, he was also a very strident supporter of the Black race and strongly identified with Liberia, as he stated:

> It is common now-a-days to hear this little Republic referred to as evidencing the incapacity of the Negro Race for free government! And nothing is more constant, nothing more frequent that the declaration that "Liberia is a failure!"

> No I venture to say—and I say it without the least hesitation, that nothing can be more ignorant, nothing more stupid than these utterances: whether they slip from the pens of Civilians, or drop from the lips of grave Senators in the Halls of Congress.[56]

Payne could be confident that his work at the school would be left with strong leadership in a person such as Crummel.

Although Payne accepted the call to Israel AME Church, in the back of his mind, he intended to return to his school. Another crucial factor in accepting a short assignment might have been Payne's reluctance to go to the nation's capital because it was still a slave territory and he had vowed upon leaving South Carolina due to the very issue of slavery that he would not return to a slave state again. In order for him to work in the District after accepting the call, he had to secure a bond to ensure his good behavior.[57] In this, one sees Payne's respect for Bishop Morris Brown.

Payne's years in the nation's capital as pastor to Israel Church were productive despite the initial confrontation over the racial divide. In order for Payne to pursue his calling to the church, he had to comply with the law that demanded his posting a bond of one thousand dollars.[58] Israel Church was a large edifice, but the congregants were too poor to place seats within it. With Payne's skills for carpentry which he learned during his teen years in Charleston, South Carolina, he reflected, "I laid aside my books, bought a jack-plane, smoothing-plane, saw, hammer, rule, etc., threw off my coat, and the Society furnishing the lumber, in a few weeks I fully seated the basement of Israel Church."[59] During this same period in time, Payne initiated the first Pastoral Association among Blacks in the community and became a public spokesperson and writer on education through essays which were published in the denomination's magazine.

EDUCATION AND MINISTRY

In that first volume of the AME Magazine which began publication in 1843, Payne wrote a series of five articles dealing with clergy education, more specifically, he was concerned with the need for an educated ministry. These articles emerged from a question posed by the editor, "What shall we do to aid our young men, that they may become competent for the ministry?" The editor raised the issue of candidacy. Payne felt the need to respond to the question in the series entitled, "Epistles on the Education for the Ministry."[60]

In the first essay, Payne identifies the causes for incompetency by some of the clergy. While the Book of Discipline of the AME Church asks candidates whether they are open to devote themselves to God and God's work, they are not asked, in Payne's words, and equally important question, "Are you resolved to qualify yourself for the work of God, in the sphere of the ministry, by making use of every literary as well as moral means?[61] Although the candidate is expected to know the doctrine of the AME Church, church history with emphasis on AME Church history, Payne makes specific curricular suggestions which include the following requirements: English Grammar, Geography, Intellectual Philosophy, Moral Philosophy, Natural and Revealed Theology. These were the requisite core for understanding for what the Book of Discipline required. In addition, Payne identifies the lack of a rigorous examination of the candidates by the examiners as a second cause, along with the way in which there are those ministers who voiced contempt for solid education for ministry.

In the second essay, Payne continues with the causes for incompetency and suggests a way to remove the causes. He identifies the fourth cause as the self-belief that some ministers consider themselves "inspired." With that being the case, "they conclude that they are infallible, and hence need neither learning nor study."[62] For Payne, they are deceiving themselves, for "inspiration" is that divine aid which enables persons to make salvation known without the possibility of error. However, the errors and mistakes are heard on most Sundays with these ministers. The fifth cause for incompetency, in Payne's opinion, was making false interpretations of scripture; he calls for a proper distinction between lase and gospel. In order to correct the situation Payne calls on the General Conference, which is the highest ecclesiastical and legislative gathering with the responsibility of governance, to address the issues at the next meeting which was scheduled to take place in May of 1844. His concern was not for making legislative decisions for themselves, but for the future of the church. Payne emphasized to the church leadership "…we are to make such as will indicate to posterity that we, their progenitors, contemplated their highest good and greatest improvement.[63]

Payne identified, in the third epistle, the second level of ecclesial authority as the Annual Conferences of the AME Church, for these gatherings have the responsibility for the examination of the local candidates. "Let them be rigid in their examination of the candidates, and never send them forth as travelling preachers, or graduate them to holy orders, until they have perfect knowledge of those branches of sacred and ecclesiastical learning which the Discipline demands." Payne declared.[64] While there was opposition to such stringent matters, Payne shared the thoughts of a candidate who was denied approval the previous year. The writer, identified as Mr. Hammonds wrote, "I have bought the books which you recommended, and have availed myself of the opportunity of which you were the cause and have had the pleasure of being examined in Dr. Schmucker's Popular Theology as far as the 131st page. I must say as an individual that I am much pleased, and if the Lord should permit me and you to see each other again, I shall have passed through the work."[65] Payne continued on to other levels of theological encounters by candidates and mentions the role of the Quarterly Conference from which those desirous of preaching and exhorting must acquire their licenses. Here he pointed to the responsibility of the Elders. The Classses are the pivotal classes where the basic theological, biblical, and doctrinal education should take place, specifically with strong study of the Bible and the *Book of Discipline*. However, very often the leadership of the Classes is not qualified for the task. It is also in the preaching that parishioners should hear the significance of ministerial education. Lastly, Payne advocated for the publication of articles dealing with the educated ministry issue.

Payne's fourth essay emphasized the examination of candidates for the Itinerancy; the traveling of the preacher from place to place.[66] Although the

Book of Discipline calls for it, there was no explicit indication of the content of the examination. Payne suggested the following courses for license should be required: Smith's *English Grammar*, Mitchell's *Geography, Sacred Geography with Ancient and Modern History*; the disciplines and doctrines of the AME church, Dr. Bangs' *Original Church of Christ* and his *History of the M.E. Church*, and Watson's *Life of Wesley*.[67] Payne pushed further with his recommendations for a four year Ordination track which included:

First year: Evidences of Divine Revelation, Sacred Canon, Introduction to the Study of the Old and New Testament, Biblical Archeology, Hermeneutics, and Compositions.

Second year: Mental and Moral Philosophy, Butler's Analogy, Schmucker's *Popular Theology*, and compositions.

Third Year: Review of the previous three years and analyses of the areas.[68]

For Payne, having studied these subject areas and not having any formal classroom experience, in four years, the church would see a change.

The fifth and concluding essay by Payne advocated the study of Hebrew and Greek. There were some who might complain about the recommendation because they didn't see themselves as linguists and regarded the appropriation of the languages as better suited for those who were in college studies. Payne repudiates this attitude because he noted that they should read the life of the Rev. John Brown of Haddington, Scotland and they would acknowledge the fact that a college education is not necessary. One notes that Payne doesn't mention his own self-education and his example of learning languages. For him, the importance of language study assisted the candidates in reading the Bible without bad translations. His plea is similar to Martin Luther, who in addition to being a theological reformer, also advocated the study of languages for apprehension of the Word in the sermon.[69] Cognizant of the number of men already in public ministry, the course recommendations were designed for those who had families and were established in ministry. However, Payne encouraged those who were young candidates for ordination to enroll and follow the college curriculum so that "the may obtain a thorough education, and enjoy all those advantages for intellectual and moral culture which result from a learned and pious faculty, philosophical apparatus, and a valuable library and which they can never enjoy outside of a college.[70] Also realizing the financial support needed for such an education, Payne planned for raising funds to support these young people including: the establishment of educational societies in congregations, special scholarship Sunday sermons, and the establishment of seminaries in the various conferences with a

comprehensive curriculum. With the last of the five epistles, Payne signs off
with the words, 'Yours for a wise and holy Ministry.'"[71] For him, these are
certainly the goals for ministry in the AME Church.

In each, he emphasized the importance of ministerial education, however,
with the publication of these epistles, there was immediate negative response,
even to the point of calling Payne a "devil" and other epithets.[72] It is also fair
to say, nonetheless, that Payne also had supporters form among the clergy;
the most important and influential of all was Bishop Morris Brown who encouraged Payne to attend the General Conference though Payne was reluctant
to participate due to the response to this essays. Brown felt that his absence
would feed into the opposition's camp. Payne acquiesced and attended the
General Conference of 1844 where Brown appointed him chair of the Committee on Education.[73] It was at the Conference that Payne introduced a resolution for a course of study for an educated ministry. He didn't expound on
the resolution, thinking that is was clear, understandable, and adequate for the
needs of the church. The discussion which followed indicated that a number
of the delegates did not side with Payne. In fact, when the vote was taken, the
resolution was defeated. Having Payne present the resolution apparently only
put fuel on the fire of resistance by the anti-education faction of the delegates.
After all, there was already a backlash from his essays in the denomination's
magazine. The next day, however, at the opening of the next session, an
A.D. Lewis, a clergyman and eloquent speaker asked that the resolution be
reconsidered. With eloquent words and an appeal to the delegates' emotions,
by the end of his speech, the words which were heard from the voters were,
"Give us the resolution, give us the resolution." It was passed unanimously.
Then, as Chair, Payne presented a course of study for the exhorters and the
pastors. The exhorters' two year program included the following fin the first
year of studies: Bible, Smith's *English Grammar*, Mitchell's *Geography*, the
AME *Book of Discipline*, and Wesley's *Notes*. In the second year of studies
the curriculum included: Original Church of Christ, History of the Methodist
Episcopal Church, and Watson's *Life of Wesley*.[74]

The course of study program for those who intended to become pastors
included in the first year: Smith's *English Grammar*, Mitchell's *Geography*,
Paley's *Evidences of Divine Revelation*, History of the Bible, Home's *Introduction*. In the second year students studied: Schmucker's *Popular Theology*,
Schmucker's *Mental Philosophy*, Natural Theology or Watson's *Institutes*.
In the third year the courses included: Ecclesiastical History, Goodrich's
Church History, Porter's *Homiletics*, and D'Aubigne's *History of the Reformation*. The final fourth year students studied Geography and Chronology of
the Bible and a review of the previous years.[75]

If one looks at the approved course of study and at the recommendations
for an educated ministry which Payne proposed in his published five essays

on education, one finds a striking similarity in the curricula. One wonders whether Bishop Brown had a planned strategy for getting the General Conference to approve the courses of study and thereby giving approval to the educational emphasis of Payne. Whatever the behind the scenes strategies that might have occurred, there was now an approved course of study for AME candidates for ministry.

In 1845, after two years in the District of Columbia, Payne was transferred to Bethel Church in Baltimore, Maryland where he was assigned for the next five years. It was an active congregation with a membership between one thousand and fifteen hundred congregants. His education interest and reputation as a teacher followed him to Bethel. Payne recalled that the wife of a local clergyman asked him whether he might be able to be the teacher for their older children. Taking his pastoral responsibilities seriously, Payne felt that the demands of the congregation and pastoral office would not allow him time to also undertake the role of "school-master." However, cognizant of his responsibilities, the woman must have been persuasive because Payne agreed to teach her children during the morning hours. Soon requests came from other families as well; consequently in a year's time Payne had dual responsibilities: he was a school-master as well as pastor of the congregation. Payne had an established school for about fifty students.

The curriculum included English studies, Greek, Latin, along with religious instruction. A Christian code of conduct ruled in the classroom. Payne exclaimed that "Law and order reigned supreme."[76] What was good for the students was beneficial for the pastor as well. Payne's daily routine consisted of teaching 9 to 2 PM; lunch; pastoral visits until tea. He retired for bed around 10 PM and was up at 5 AM in order to study to again at 9 AM. In addition to visiting parishioners, preaching the Word and teaching students, Payne demonstrated his interest and ability in the worship life of the congregation.

It was at Bethel that instrumental music was introduced into the AME Church. The circumstances for this addition to the worship life came in 1848 with the building of a new edifice, the payment on the fifteen thousand dollar mortgage, and the need to begin payment of the note of ten thousand dollars. Securing the time and talent of Dr. James Fleet, a noted musician for a concert of sacred music, Payne had a concert of sacred music to raise the funds for the mortgage. He composed words to assure theological and biblical appropriateness for the church setting. In another concert, there was another success, with the addition of seven stringed instruments under the podium of Mr. William Appo, an accomplished Black musician.[77] With financial as well as musical innovation, members of the congregation were able to see that instrumental music could be used for religious purposes and the enhancement of the community's worship life. For Payne, these musical additions to the service were an extension of the pulpit, an extension of the Word of God for the people of God:

A choir, with instruments as an accompaniment, can be made a powerful and efficient auxiliary to the pulpit. Two things are essential to the saving power and efficiency of choral music—a scientific training and an earnest Christianity. Two things are necessary to make choral singing always profitable to a Church—that the congregation shall always join in singing with the choir, and that they shall always sing with the spirit and the understanding.[78]

The use of music, vocal and instrumental, had a teaching function in the church as well. As women and men are nurtured on spoken words in the sermons, so too, the use of choral and instrumental music brings together the gifts of God. Payne makes his case:

Man is a product of God's wisdom and power; therefore, he should be called upon to praise God with his mouth. The instruments are the product of man's genius and skill. Why not use the sounds of these instruments to praise the Creator?[79]

In order to do all of this, we can readily see that Payne was disciplined and organized. He remembered his schedule.

His assignment to Bethel was a three-church charge. Payne had responsibilities for three churches, going to them by horseback, but it was burdensome for one person, and he asked Bishop Morris Brown to be relieved of some of the responsibilities. In response to his request, the bishop divided the parish into two (Bethel as one with Ebenezer and Union Bethel on Fell's Point as the other). Payne notes that despite the heavy workload, there was a steady growth in the membership at Bethel.

In July of 1846 Payne's world view began to expand. He was designated from Bethel, along with Rev. Clark, an associate delegate of the New York Conference of the AME Church, to be a delegate to the meeting of the Evangelical Alliance.[80] The two intended to venture to Europe for the initial meeting of the organization to be held in London, England.

The Evangelical Alliance was an international, inter-denominational organization, a predecessor ecumenical body of the now World Council of Churches. One of the leaders in its formation was Samuel Simon Schmucker, Payne's former professor and the president of Gettysburg Seminary. It is not surprising that Payne became interested in the area of church life as well. Schmucker's interest in ecumenical ministry emerged from several points including his evangelization, the rise of Roman Catholicism, and mission outreach. His ecumenical efforts span about thirty-five years, with several publication. Most notably during the Payne period were "Fraternal Appeal to the American Churches, with a Plan for Catholic Union, on Apostolic Principles" in published in 1838 and "Overture for Christian Union, Submitted for the Consideration of the Evangelical Denominations in the United States" in 1846. This "Overture" which had been shared with peers in North America and Europe brought Schmucker a personal invitation to the first meeting of what was then called the World's Evangelical Alliance to take place in London from August 19 through September 2 in 1846. This was the culmination of several smaller meetings that had been held in various parts of Europe in which Schmucker's "Appeal" had been noticed and discussed. Schmucker departed from the United States in April of 1846 to take an extended tour of Europe before arriving at the meeting. His former student and now pastor in the African Methodist Episcopal Church, Daniel Payne, departed from Baltimore in July of 1846 for the same meeting.

The initial days of the trip went well. Payne even remarked to a fellow passenger just how remarkable the weather was after two days on the ocean. But his remarks were premature, for on about the fifth day a storm developed, and in the middle of the night passengers were awakened, sails were damaged, and some of the crew lost their lives. They were ferried back to shore, as they were only about 500 miles from their point of departure. Although Payne's fellow colleague, Clark, mad the voyage to Europe on the next departing ship, Payne decided not to go. One reason for his change of mind was presented to him in a dream in which he saw himself addressing delegates at the "Alliance" meeting against slavery so strongly that he could not return to the States for fear for his life. He concluded, "As I look back I can but feel that such a course was better, as I certainly should have denounced slavery in no measured terms, and in the excited state of the minds of the people for and against the system the whole current of my life's work would undoubtedly have been changed, if indeed I had not most my life altogether.[81]

Indeed, the issue of slavery had surfaced at the London meeting. It became one of the sticky points for church unity in terms of membership in the organization. Some delegates wanted a qualifier for membership, indicating that slaveholders could not be members, while some others felt that it was not a part of the discussion. Schmucker, always the moderate was not an advocate for their exclusion. For that would be too divisive.[82] On this point, the teacher and former student would likely to have been on opposite ends of the issue.

Although the voyage was aborted, Payne did experience life on the ship. Payne was in conversation with an Irish-American merchant from Payne's place of birth, Charleston, South Carolina, whom he describes as "cheerful and kind." Payne remembers Charleston as "that hospitable, beautiful, romantic, city, where repose in heavenly quietude the sacred ashes of my sainted parents."[83] Along with a variety of people aboard the ship there were also included a variety of attitudes. One incident involved the ever-present racism on the part of some white Americans which Payne identifies. In a specific incident, a Kentucky slave-holder commented in a loud voice, "'is that nigger holding forth there?'"[84] A further incident of American racism which was more institutional than personal was demonstrated by the treatment of Blacks in the matter related to accommodations. Payne wrote:

> In regard to our treatment on board the vessel at that time, I am sorry to say that American prejudice marked us out here as elsewhere, reminding us that we were still in a country where the standard of manhood was the color of the skin, the proof of which is this: After paying seventy-five dollars, the same price that others paid who had state-rooms and every comfort in them, with the untrammeled used of the cabin, we were placed in the steward's quarters, situated between the first and second cabin, with no seat but our trunks, no towels, no looking-glass, no soap, bowls, or any necessary convenience. In regard to our eating, the rule here was reversed; and, instead of giving us our food when the cabin passengers had finished, we had ours first of all. This cruel spirit caused us to fervently desire a swift and safe voyage to the true 'land of the free and the home of the brave.'[85]

His reference to "land of the free and home of the brave" is to England where, he notes, "a man is not held in contempt and ostracized on account of his color, but is honored on account of character and usefulness in the land from whence he comes.[86] The abolition of slavery in England and within its colonies ended in 1833 through the Slavery Abolition Act 1833.

Following the attempted voyage and Payne's reluctance to return on the ship, he continued to grow personally and professionally in the church. Two years, later at the 1848 General Conference of the AME Church, Payne was appointed historiographer of the church.[87] It is also significant, at the same meeting, the Conference addressed the need and plan for the common schools within the church, "The pastor of every church was empowered to establish a high school wherever practicable, provided that the Annual Conference approved and sanctioned such a measure in their respective districts." Furthermore, the importance of an educated ministry was upheld with the revision of the course of study adopted at the General Conference of 1844. Young men were asked to become "proficient" or not be able to advance in "holy orders"[88] The educational initiative was becoming a priority for the leadership.

While Payne's contribution and rise in the AME Church was becoming more pronounced, he also met with emotional turmoil. In 1847, a year after the aborted trip to Europe, he married Julia A. Ferris of Washington, DC. However, marital bliss was brief, as she died that same year, a few hours after the birth of a daughter. Payne described his inner turmoil in his poem, "My Julia:"

Though art gone to the Land of rest!
Art gone to the home of the pure!
Thou are gone to the Heavenly rest,
Thy Saviour and God to adore.

Thou art gone from this region of death,
Where sorrow and suffering are rife,
To the clime whose ethereal breath
Give pleasure and rapture to life.

Thou art gone from thy kindred below,
To join thy relation in Heaven,
Where the temple, the heart and the glow,
O friendship and dewdrop are giv'n.

Thou art gone from the cross to the crown!
From work to the glorious reward.
From the prisoner's chain to the conqueror's throne!
From my arms to the bosom of God.

Thou art gone not as dreams of night,
Nor shadows that fly o're the glade —
For thy image, immortal, and bright,
Is seen in my angelic babe.

Like the wild worm which weaves its own shroud,
And dies to give birth to its' fly —
So didst thou; then upon a bright cloud,
Thou are gone to the mansions on high.

Where the seraphim's glorious voice,
And the harps of the saints do resound;
Thou art gone, O my love to rejoice
With Angels, in glory, life-crowned.[89]

Further tragedy occurred with their daughter's death on 12 July 1848, after living only nine months. Payne wrote the following lines:

Another painful blow is struck,
The golden chain again is riv'n
The link which bound my heart to earth
Is broke, and fasten'd now to heaven.

Behold! My cherub child is gone!
On wings, whose plumes are beams of light,

Through on blue sky by babe has blown
With angels fair and seraphs bright.

They came at the eve of the day;
When the sheen of the sun is mild,
In cars of light they bore away
By beauteous daughter—cherub child!

But the blooms in a brighter clime,
Where all is pure and sweet and green,
Where dark disease and storms of time
Are neither felt, nor beard, nor seen.

I mourn not for thee, sweetest on;
Though wert loan'd, but never were giv'n
Bright gem from the land of the sun,
Go shine mist the jewels of heav'n!

And O! when this short life is o'er;
When this frail form is laid in dust;
Swift up to heav'n my soul shall soar
To meet the!—angel child—I must![90]

Despite the turmoil of grief, his duties as pastor of Ebenezer as well as the responsibility as Historiographer of the AME Church continued, however, the reception that Payne received by members of the congregation was less than welcoming. Although they didn't find fault with his character, the circulated a variety of false stories; from relating his style of living to the way in which he furnished his home; from his being a proud person to his not being hospitable. Perhaps the crowning blow was his disallowing them to sing "spirited songs" at worship.[91]

Payne countered these allegations by stating that he declined their dinner invitations when they conflicted with other pressing pastoral duties. He countered their comments on his restriction on worship music by stating that they were primarily interested in using song forms the "corn-field ditties" variety. This attack on his pastoral authority was very difficult for Payne, and he ended his pastoral relationship with the congregation through Bishop Quinn though Bishop Quinn urged otherwise. Payne declined the request stating that if they did not want him, he didn't want them. Although the pastoral duties ended, Payne was able to give more time and energy to his responsibilities as historiographer of the AME Church and to the task of writing the history of the denomination.

In May of 1849, Bishop Morris Brown, a great supporter of Payne, died and Payne delivered the sermon at the funeral. Although Bishop Brown was not literate, he supported the efforts of those who had those abilities. It was Brown who urged Payne to attend and propose his educational vision to the General Conference, and again Brown who had appointed Payne to the Education Task Force of the church as well. With this in mind, Payne remembered Brown with these words,

> As the Bishop never had so much as a primary-school education, it cannot be expected that he should have left any personal records of his labors, nor the exercises of his mind upon the various subjects which daily engrossed his attention as the Bishop of the A. M. E. Church. We, and all who knew him, can truthfully say, that notwithstanding all the literary disadvantages under which he labored, he was, in spirit, abreast of the age, and to the utmost of his knowledge and power encouraged the education of his people. We can furnish no greater evidence of this than where he is seen refusing to ordain a young itinerant because he had not the literary qualifications required by the Discipline.[92]

Payne's research on the church's history required him to travel to AME ministry sites in the Eastern and Western States, as well as southwest to New Orleans and north into Canada. During his travels in New England he also visited and surveyed cemeteries or "cities of the dead." He recalled vividly, while in New Haven, visiting the grave of Noah Webster, "the greatest lexicographer that ever lived," with its granite obelisk. Of equal importance to Payne was his visit to Yale College, in New Haven, Connecticut; he remarks upon leaving the State and College,

> One century and a half have seen thee preparing the minds which are to give character to the American Church and the American State, and thou art still destined to affect the lengthening, widening States for weal or for woe. Thy State, as well as thy college, was founded by the heralds of the cross. Go tell thy statesmen to wipe from their Constitution and statutes those laws which persecute the hapless sons of Ham, and thou shalt be just what a Christian State ought to be. Farewell![93]

In Boston he visited Mount Auburn cemetery where he was moved again, as with his memory of Webster's tomb, but his time by an abolitionist, Charles Torrey, who had been arrested for assisting a fugitive slave. He was not given a pardon even on the brink of his death in a Southern jail. Payne had known, written to, and warned him about the danger and threat to his life undertaking this task. But Payne noted his commitment to the liberation of blacks in slavery. On his monument was also the figure of a female slave with the following words above her,

> Where now beneath his burden
> The toiling slave is driven,
> Where now a tyrant's mockery
> Is offered up to heaven:
> Then shall his praise be spoken,
> Redeemed from falsehood's ban
> When the fetters shall be broken,
> And the slave shall be a man.[94]

One notices the dual role that Payne had taken upon himself: the writer of history and religious life within the church, as well as the chronicler of the state of his black brothers and sister under the reign of slavery. He saw the power of education as the means of exposing the gaps in the American social system when he remembers his visit to Yale. He observed the fate of persons dedicated to the cause of freedom and the sacrifices that people made prior to the lives taken during the Civil War two decades later.

During the fall of 1850 and the winter of 1851, Payne concentrated his research efforts in the state of Pennsylvania, although in the summer he crossed over into Ohio and ventured down to Cincinnati. Commenting and reflecting on the trip which was arduous by ship, Payne lifted up a prayer, "Make, O make me a faithful minister and teacher, so that I may guide both young and old into the way everlasting, and see everyone who has ever been committed to my care lodged in the kingdom of God![95] Commitment to Word and Sacrament ministry as pastor; Word and Service ministry as teacher; Payne balances his love and commitment to both. Payne returned by a northern route stopping in Columbus, Cleveland, Ohio and back to Pennsylvania where he attended the opening of the academic year at Allegheny Institute and heard its founder, the Rev. Charles Avery.[96] Charles Avery was born in West Chester, Pennsylvania and was advised to go west, where he relocated in Pittsburgh in 1812. He began his accumulation of wealth by opening a drugstore since he had been apprenticed to a druggist in New York City. With his surplus profits, he ventured into the cotton industry where he amassed much wealth. On visiting in the southern United States, he saw the devastating effects of slavery on blacks, and that exposure turned him to the abolitionist movement. Avery became so immersed that he helped slaves escape by the underground railroad from the south to Canada. In addition, he also became interested in the education of Black and founded Allegheny Institute and Mission Church which were incorporated in 1849. The curriculum included six departments: Manuel training, domestic economy, millinery, tailoring, literary, and public schooling. Tuition was free to students.

Payne admired Avery not only for his abolitionist efforts and educational endeavor on the behalf of the black women and men but also for his piety. To be admitted to the school, the student was required to bring a certificate indicating the student's good moral character; and those students transferring to the Institute had to have affidavits of honorable dismissal from the former institution.[97]

Payne noted and admired Avery's work on behalf of the women and men of color. He was taken by Avery's stewardship of resources for the elimination of illiteracy among them.[98] Payne goes on to state,

> He that takes the rough marble out of the quarry and by his plastic genius forms it into a beautiful statue performs a great work and excites the admiration of all posterity; but he who takes the rude, unlettered mind, and molds it into the educated, refined, intellectual, and moral image of the Deity performs a work a thousand times greater and excites the admiration of eternity, the praise of angels, and the approval of his God. I would rather be Charles Avery than Julius Cæsar or Napoleon Bonaparte.[99]

Although Payne had a busy travel schedule due to his dedication and commitment to the research task, he had to also support himself since he was not involved as a parish pastor. To support himself Payne he went on the lecture circuit giving talks in the area of stewardship, i.e. "Industry and Thrift," "The Springs of Wealth." Always the creative and innovative teacher, he used visuals to enhance and complement his lectures.[100]

In April of 1852, he returned home in Baltimore, only to then turn around again to go to New York for the General Conference at Old Bethel Church, where another milestone in his life was to take place. The conference began on May 3, with Payne preaching at the opening Service. His sermon based on II Corinthians 2:16 "... to the one a fragrance from death to death, to the other a fragrance from life to life. Who is sufficient for these things?" was entitled, "Who is sufficient for these things?" Incorporated into his sermon was his educational theme:

> Sufficiency is not to be found in man, but in God... Is man a mere passive being in the matter; or does God require some action on his part? We answer, in this respect man is not like a seed placed in the ground, which can be developed by the morning and evening dews, together with the native warmth of the earth and the sunbeams. He must use the mind that God has given him; he must cultivate this mind, and seek that aid which is given to every one whom he has called to the work of the ministry.

He goes on to say, "First, then, let him cultivate his mind by all the means in his power. With the light of science, philosophy and literature, let him illumine his understanding, and carry this culture and this illumination to the highest point possible." Payne was quick to point out that this attitude was not shared by all and related a portion from his life experience:

> Now, it is for teaching sentiments like these that I have been slandered, perse-cuted and hated. This has been the head and front of my offending. But brethren, am I not right? Is it not proper that I should seek the improvement of those who had not the chance of an early education? Yes; I have done it, and still will seek the improvement of all my young brethren, that they may be both intelligent, well educated and holy men.[101]

ELECTION TO BISHOP

One of the major decisions for the delegates at the Conference that would prove to be significant and life-changing for Payne and the AME Church was his nomination and election to the office of Bishop. However, this was not the first time that Payne's name was mentioned as a possible bishop in the AME Church. His name was recommended at the General Conference of 1848, only seven years after he became a member of that denomination. What was the difference that caused him to accept the nomination at this Conference? This time, on 7 May 1852, Payne felt the call of God upon him, and for him to refuse the call to his way of thinking, would not be pleasing to the "Great Head of the Church." He said simply, "I yielded because I felt that the omnipotent Arm that had thrust me into the position would hold me in it."[102] Payne felt unfit and unsuited for this level of ministry, but others only saw his gifts for ministerial leadership as a Bishop of the Church. On 13 May, Payne and William Nazrey of Philadelphia were ordained Bishops.[103]

It is interesting to note that among the invited ecumenical guests at the Conference was the Rev. Charles Avery, whom Payne had encountered four years previously. Payne summarized Avery's address in which he stated that he,

> ...felt grateful to God for the privilege he enjoyed of speaking in the presence of the Conference. He spoke of the Allegheny Institute as a place of learning for the colored youth of this country; that a complete course of classical education could be obtained there. He said that his hopes were, that in the further progress of his college, young men would be educated for usefulness in the ministry, in schools, and other colleges, etc., and concluded by urging upon the ministers the importance of using their influence among the people, by encouraging them to send their children to schools and to college. He thought the great aims of the Church should be, first, to educate the young men for the ministry, and, second, to educate the entire community for usefulness in society; for our only hope of future elevation under God depended upon this.[104]

The newly elected Bishop Payne was called on to respond to Avery. Payne stated that to be among a people with rights and privileges within this nation, it was imperative that we become educated. Again, he used a portion of his own history and his encounter with the gentleman from North Carolina who challenged him to consider the difference between the master and the slave. Payne stated,

> Said he, "Daniel, do you know what makes the master and servant? Nothing but superior knowledge—nothing but one man knowing more than another. Now, if you will go with me, the knowledge you may acquire will be of more value to you than three hundred dollars"—the amount of the salary promised by him. Immediately I seized the idea. Instead of going to travel as his servant, I went and chained my mind down to the study of science and philosophy, that I might obtain that knowledge which makes the master.[105]

He summed up his response by saying,

> You, Reverend Sir, are the founder of this institution. The sculptor who takes the rude marble out of the quarry and carves it into a beautiful human figure, immortalizes himself by enshrining his genius in the almost breathing statue, and to him the praise of mankind is due... It now remains for us to do all that is in our power, which is: First, to tender, in the name of our hapless race, our unfeigned thanks for your noble efforts to educate it; and secondly, to do our utmost to promote its prosperity.[106]

How appropriate and fortuitous that Avery was present at the Conference and ordination. Avery's presence and Payne's response as a new Bishop of the church indicated the direction and tone of Payne's leadership as bishop. One recalls his first message on behalf of education under the leadership of Bishop Quinn. While his formal address upon being elected took place later, there is the sense in which these words marked the beginning of his tenure as Bishop and educational leader in the church.

In the initial years in the bishop's office Payne continued to travel; however, his primary task was that of shepherd to members of his Episcopal District. With three bishops for the church, the geographic areas of responsibility had to be divided among the men. Payne was assigned to the First District which comprised the Philadelphia and New England Conferences.

As can be imagined, Payne took his responsibilities seriously and visited the churches in the two areas. But his title did not automatically open doors for him. He remarked that he was refused plain hospitality by members of his own denomination who were used to hosting traveling clergy. A significant aspect of Payne's self-identity emerges here; what counts is not the weight of the office of Bishop, but the need of the stranger to be welcomed.

One year later, on 16 May 1853, Payne made his first address as Bishop at the Philadelphia Annual Conference.[107] His concern for the educational strength of the church continued what began the previous year in his response to Charles Avery. Payne saw the need for more schools as he ventured in the Philadelphia area and competent trained teachers as well to fill the need. In addition, he called on pastors in his district to focus on education in their preaching. They should have a sermon on the issue the family and religion at least every six months. Parents need to send and keep their children in school up to and including high school to reap the advantages. Moreover, they should take advantage of the library where the availability of books makes education accessible to parents and children without cost. In addition, congregants have and should continue to attend the scientific lectures delivered by knowledgeable professional men and women.

Bishop Payne also identified three obstacles: a large rate of illiteracy among the constituency which means, little or no support for the denomination's newspaper or other publications; lack of financial support which would allow the church to publish more literature; and apathy on the part of those in itinerant ministry.

He also addressed the need for competent Sunday school teachers and suggested that they meet once a week for their own continuing education. These teachers should be provided books for their educational uplift: Bible Geography, Bible Dictionary, Natural History of the Bible, Nevins' Biblical Antiquities, New Bible Atlas, maps, etc. For Payne, these elements will assist the teachers in making "the schools places of attraction and delight; and thus, under the influences of the Holy Spirit, the Sunday school will become the garden in which plants shall be cultivated to bloom forever amid the paradise of God."[108]

Payne not only saw the need for an educated ministry in terms of clergy preparation but also for their continuing education after they were engaged in ministry. He spoke directly to his clergy and recommended that they devote three hours a day cultivating the intellect. He encouraged the clergy to study the languages: Hebrew, Greek, and Latin, if they have not previously.

In addition to such internal concerns in the bishop's address, Payne also expressed concerns about the relationship between the church membership and the state or country. The church is not the same as the living God. There is good and bad in all governments. He further stated that the American government was an oppressor as it enslaves those with even a drop of African blood as well as chases and hunts down those who attempt to flee. Moreover, the governmental form doesn't mean anything but the execution of just laws and an impartial administration at the service of freedom and equality.

In sum, for Payne, knowledge was power. Such knowledge can serve the most influential institution on North American soil for people of color, the church.

The bishop re-emphasized education in his travels and drew public attention. During one of his visits to New York, he met with Lewis Tappen, the philanthropist, who introduced him to Myrtle Miner who desired to meet him. The meeting was helpful. She had the passion for teaching and desired to go to Washington, D.C. to open a high school for Black girls. Her determination moved Payne to give her letters of introduction to the prominent Black families in the city including that of his sister-in-law of the Becraft family. In turn, these families provided Miner with her first pupils for the opening of the Miner Normal School. In 1853, Payne visited the school describing the teaching method as one that "developed all the faculties of the soul."[109]

Miner was a native New Yorker who opened her school on 6 December 1851. She was driven by the conviction that Blacks had the intellectual abilities and capacities to learn, but oppression had limited their progress. She began the school with only six students, but by the time Payne saw her in two years later, the school had an enrollment of about forty students.[110] Although she experienced much hostility in her desire to open a school, Miner was committed to the task. This demonstration of perseverance would resonate with Payne.

In the fall of October 12 in 1854, Payne married for the second time.[111] His new spouse was Mrs. Eliza J. Clark, a widow with children, who lived in Cincinnati, Ohio. Payne moved West, but his place of residence was not that significant in that he had responsibilities in that area since he was in charge of the Ohio Conference at that time. His travels and administrative tasks continued: settling conflicts in congregations, racial tensions in congregations, expulsion of a pastor, and taking on additional responsibilities when Bishop Quinn was severely beaten by robbers and was unable to function for several months. Doing double duty didn't fare well with Payne's physical well-being, and he was ill due to "prostration of the nervous system" and was unable to do any public speaking for several months.

After his recuperation, during one of his pastoral trips in 1855 Payne stopped in Springfield, Ohio. There he visited his former classmate, Dr. Samuel Sprecher. Sprecher was a member of the mission society which had sponsored Payne while at Gettysburg, the society he also joined. The scope of Payne's conversation with Sprecher dealt with the plight of Blacks both within the United States and in Africa.[112] At the time of his visit, Sprecher was President of Wittenberg College, a position which he held from 1849 through 1874.[113]

Payne also had the opportunity to visit and talk with Victor Conrad, editor of the *Evangelical Lutheran*. Their discussion centered on the emancipation of the slaves as well as the moral effects of this institution on the slaves and the slaveholders. Payne was very enthusiastic about the positions that he held.

Conrad was also a Gettysburg graduate and licensed in 1851. In addition to these personal visits, Payne also addressed an integrated and ecumenical gathering of the Sunday School Society in Springfield.

Coupled with Payne's visits to friends, acquaintances and church members, there were also serious issues that had to be addressed by the church. Ever aware of the racism that existed in the country, he expected the church to exhibit the qualities that countered the social limitations of the general society. As racism existed and was the cause for the formation of the AMEC at St. George Church, it was also exhibited within the congregations of the AMEC. That was intolerable to Payne and took measures against such attitudes in the churches within his jurisdiction. An example of this occurred in Philadelphia in 1853 a year after his election as Bishop. A Caucasian woman opened a school for the education of Black children. Such an action did not make her welcome in many circles of white society and she began to worship at Bethel AME where many of her students' parents were members. She joined a class meeting which was met with ire by the female members of the church. Payne related that a gentleman from the congregation asked whether there were any prohibitions in the *Book of Discipline* concerning white membership in AMEC congregations. Payne responded with a definitive "NO!" and added that Christianity "is open to all and for all." The pastor of the congregation ultimately barred the woman from the church. In Payne's response to that action, we see the authority of the Bishop's office and the commitment of the Bishop to the "doing" of the gospel; Payne, stated, "My sense of duty in this case led me to leave that pastor without an appointment at the next Annual Conference. This caused much excitement among his personal friends, and I was urged to change my purpose; but to all I firmly replied that I feared not the result."[114]

In consultation with the other Bishops whether they should employ the pastor, Payne stated, "I replied that they might do whatever they thought proper in the case, but I believed that the pastor who would turn away from God's sanctuary any human being on account of color was not fit to have charge of a gang of dogs."[115] The incident underscores Payne's commitment to racial inclusivity in the church and in general. For Payne, the gospel clearly and definitively dissolved the visible distinctions which divided humankind. It was incumbent upon the church to exhibit that which the nation could not.

In 1855, in another incident, illustrative of racial issues in the church, Payne was the one who felt the brunt of discrimination. He was preaching and lecturing at a Methodist Episcopal church in Bloomington, IL where the pastor did not show hospitality by any stretch of the imagination. He refused to accompany Payne to the pulpit. After announcing the offering that would be collected for Payne, he left the church before Payne descended. Payne could only comment, "I suppose he was laboring under the influence of slave-hold-ers, or that legitimate offspring of slave-holders—American prejudice."[116]

As Payne experienced the hostilities and racial prejudice, one wonders, how he was able to persevere. A key to this man comes to us from his journal entry at the beginning of 1856. Payne's New Year's resolutions included his personal intentions: to be thrifty in spending, not to speak demeaning of anyone, to pay his debts as well as not acquiring new ones, and to give more in terms of benevolence.[117] In addition, Payne outlined his own theological studies of self-education which included: Read and study Paul's letter to the Romans, Schaff's *A History of the Apostolic Church, History of the Anglo-saxons*; the study of Latin and French; reading Chemistry, and work on the history of his church.[118] Moreover, he intended to visit families and the com-mon schools in the areas where he was scheduled to travel. Being centered in scripture and dedicated to life-long learning helped to keep him focused as he carried out his responsibilities as a servant-leader in the church. The follow-ing month, Payne was confronted with more personal turmoil.

In February of 1856, Payne was arrested in St. Louis for violating the laws of the state. He was arrested for preaching the Gospel. Although his friends provided the bail for him, the charges were dismissed on a technicality; the warrant was for a Thomas A. Payne and he was Daniel A. Payne. However, no sooner had Payne exited the magistrate's building than there was a new warrant for his arrest. Fortunately, a fellow clergyman, John Early, was wait-ing for him to leave and Payne was put immediately in the wagon. They left quickly with the sound of voices calling for the carriage to stop, they crossed into the free state of Illinois. The case was heard for a second time in Payne's absence and was dismissed as Payne was a free person and entitled to protec-tion of the civil authorities in the city of St. Louis.

Payne continued to be on the move following the occurrence in St. Louis. During the same summer that Payne had thought and was prepared to move to upstate New York near the Albany Manual Labor School. He felt the move would make him centrally located for his travels; however, upon a visit from representatives of the Cincinnati Conference in Ohio that anticipated the establishment of an educational institution, they invited him to visit the area. Payne visited and fell in love with the surrounding and decided to move there. On 3 July 1856, Payne made a move from Cincinnati to Tawawa Springs, Ohio the future site of the educational institution that the Methodist Episcopal Church had under consideration.

The ugly face of racism with its disruptive manifestations continued to ac-company Payne even to the end of the year. In December, on a pastoral trip to New Orleans, he could not be assured of his safety, neither by the mayor of the city nor the Episcopal Church bishop, Leonidas Polk. Both recommended that Payne leave as quickly as possible. However, Payne was made of stronger fiber and was determined to fulfill his church obligations and did not shorten his trip staying for three weeks with no incidents of racial harassment.[119]

Thus ends this phase of the life of Daniel Payne. Transition was the theme throughout this period of his life: from itinerant preacher to historiographer of the AME Church; from marriage to death of a spouse to re-marriage; from congregational pastor to bishop of the AME Church; and countless relocations. All of these changes prepared Payne for his most fruitful years as a national ecclesiastical leader and educator in the nineteenth century.

NOTES

1. Daniel A. Payne, *History of the African Methodist Episcopal* Church (Nashville, Tennessee: Publishing House of the A.M.E. Sunday-School Union, 1891. http://docsouth.unc.edu/church/payne/payne.html, 26.

2. Ibid., 262.

3. Ibid.

4. *Recollections*, 64.

5. Clifford E. Nelson, *The Lutherans in North America* rev. ed. (Philadelphia: Fortress Press, 1975, 1980), 143.

6. Franckean Synod, *Franckean Synod Minutes* (Albany: Hoffman and White, 1837), 8.

7. Ibid., 9.

8. Ibid., 22.

9. Ibid., 24.

10. Dennis Dickerson, *Religion, Race, and Region: Research Notes on A.M.E. History* (Nashville: Legacy Publishing, 1995), 37.

11. Payne, *Recollections*, 65.

12. *Franckean Synod Minutes*, 27.

13. Daniel A. Payne to the Rev. Phillip Wieting Secretary of Franckean Synod, 5 June 1838.

14. Ibid.

15. Franckean Synod. *Journal of the First Annual Session of the Franckean Synod of the Evangelic Lutheran Church Convened at Clay, Onondaga County, N.Y. June 7th, 1838* (Albany: Hoffman and White, 1838), 6.

16. Payne, *Recollections*, 66.

17. *The Minutes and Proceedings of the First Annual Meeting of the American Moral Reform Society, 14–19 August 1837*, 3 http://memory.loc.gov/cgi-bin/query/r?ammem/murray:@field(DOCID+@lit(lcrbmrpt2117div2)).

18. Ibid., 5.

19. Ibid., 19, 23, 24.

20. Ibid., 30,31.

21. Payne, *Recollections*, 67; John Hope Franklin and Alfred A. Moss, Jr. *From Slavery to Freedom*, 166.

22. Payne, *Recollections*, 67; see also, Hugh Davis, *Joshua Leavitt: Evangelical Abolitionist* (Baton Rouge: Louisiana State University, 1990).

23. Payne, *Recollections*, 67; Franklin, *From Slavery to Freedom*, 160,162.

24. Payne, *Recollections*, 67; Franklin, *From Slavery to Freedom*, 162.

25. Payne, *Recollections*, 67.

26. Ibid., 68.

27. October 7, 1837 *The Colored American*.

28. Payne, *Recollections*, 68.

29. Ibid., 70.

30. Gerrit (Philanthropist) Smith. *American National Biography*. John A. Garraty and Mark C. Carnes, eds. (New York: Oxford University Press, 1999): Gerrit Smith, *Dictionary of American Biography*. Dumas Malone, ed. (New York: Charles Scribner's Son, 1935); Ralph Volney Harlow, *Gerrit Smith: Philanthropist and Reformer* (New York: Henry Holt and Company, 1939).

31. Milton C. Sernett, *Abolition's Axe: Beriah Green, Oneida Institute, and the Black Freedom Struggle* (Syracuse: Syracuse University Press, 1986),47; see also Milton C. Sernett, "Common Cause: The Antislavery Alliance of Gerritt Smith and Beriah Green" *Syracuse University Library Associate Courier* Vol.21, no.2 (Fall 1984):55–76.

32. Franckean Synod. *Journal of the Second Annual Session of the Franckean Evangelic Lutheran Synod, Convened at Fordsboro, Montgomery Co. June 6, 1839. Minutes of the Franckean Synod* (Fort Plain: Wm.L. Fish, 1839), 17.

33. *The Lutheran Herald* July 1839; Douglas C. Stange, "Document: Bishop Daniel Alexander Payne's Protestation of American Slavery" *Journal of Negro History* 52 (1967): 59–64.

34. *The Lutheran Herald* July 1839.

35. Payne, *Recollections*, 74.

36. Payne to Schmucker, 20 March 1841.

37. Coan, 60.

38. Ibid., 61.

39. Payne, *History of the African Methodist Episcopal Church*, 141.

40. Ibid., 158; see also, The African Methodist Episcopal Church, *The Book of Discipline of the African Methodist Episcopal Church* (Nashville: AMEC Sunday School Union, 2009), 673; Ted Campbell, *Methodist Doctrine* (Nashville: Abingdon Press, 1999), 131; Thomas Edward Frank, *Journal of Religious Leadership* 5 (Spring and Fall, 2006): 109–129.

41. Payne, *History of the African Methodist Episcopal Church*, 163.

42. Charles H. Wesley, *Richard Allen Apostle of Freedom* (Washington, D.C.: The Associated Publishers, 1935), 3.

43. For extensive biographical information on Allen readers are directed to Carol V. R. George, *Segregated Sabbaths* (New York: Oxford University Press, 1973); Richard S. Newman, *Freedom's Prophet* (New York: New York University Press,

2008); Anne H. Pinn and Anthony B. Pinn, *Fortress Introduction to Black Church History* (Minneapolis: Fortress Press, 2002).

44. Richard Allen, *The Life, Experience, and Gospel Labours of the Rt. Rev. Richard Allen*, (Philadelphia: Martin & Boden, 1833), 5. http://docsouth.unc.edu/neh/allen/allen.html.

45. Ibid., 9–10.

46. Ibid., 11.

47. Ibid., 13.

48. Ibid., 15.

49. Ibid., 16.

50. Ibid., 17.

51. Ibid., 21.

52. Payne, *History*, 14.

53. Ibid., 84.

54. Ibid.

55. Franckean Synod, *Journal of the Fifth Annual Session of the Franckean Synod* 2 June 1842 (Milford, NY: Lutheran Herald Office, 1842), 24.

56. Alex Crummell, *Africa and America: Addresses and Discourses* (Springfield, MA:Willey and Co., 1891). Rep. ed. (New York: Negro Universities Press, 1969), v; *Encyclopedia of African-American Culture and History*. Jack Salzman, David Lionel Smith and Cornel West eds. Vol 2. New York: Macmillan, 1996; see also J.R. Oldfield, Alexander Crummell (1819–1898) *And the Creation of an African-American Church in Liberia* (Lewiston: the Edwin Mellen Press, 1990).

57. Payne, *Recollections*, 75; see also, Worthington Snethen, *Black Codes of the District of Columbia in force September 1, 1848* (New York: A&F Anti-Slavery Society, 1848).

58. Laws Passed by the Eighteenth Council of the City of Washington, Approved April 14, 1821, Sections 1–21 (pp.109–116); Letitia Woods Brown, *Free Negroes in the District of Columbia 1790–1846* (New York: Oxford University Press, 1922).

59. Payne, *Recollections*, 75.

60. *AME Magazine* vol.1 April 1843, 108.

61. Ibid.

62. *AME Magazine*, vol.1 July 1843, 159.

63. Ibid., 160.

64. *AME Magazine*, September 1843, 188.

65. Ibid.

66. *Book of Discipline*, 676; Campbell, 131.

67. *AME Magazine*, November 1843, 211.

68. Ibid., 211.

69. Martin Luther, "To the Councilmen in All Cities in Germany That They Establish and Maintain Christian Schools, 1524," trans. Albert T. W. Steinhaeuser, *Luther's Works* vol. 45 (Philadelphia: Muhlenberg Press, 1962),358,365.

70. *AME Magazine*, January 1844, 276.

71. Ibid., 278.

72. Payne, *Recollections*, 76.

73. Payne, *History of the AME Church*, 158; *Recollections*, 77.

74. Payne, *History of the AME Church*, 169.

75. Ibid.

76. Payne, *Recollections*, 79.

77. Ibid., 236.

78. Ibid., 237.

79. Ibid.

80. Ibid., 82.

81. Ibid., 85.

82. Abdel Ross Wentz, *Pioneer in Christian Unity: Samuel Simon Schmucker* (Philadelphia: Fortress Press, 1967; reissued 1999), 290.

83. Payne, *Recollections*, 87.

84. Ibid., 88.

85. Ibid., 90.

86. Ibid., 91.

87. Payne, *History of the AME Church*, 221.

88. Ibid., 220.

89. Coan, 73; see also Payne, *Poems of Pleasures and other Misc.* (Baltimore: Sherwood and Company, 1850), 32.

90. Ibid., Payne, *Poems*, 34.

91. Payne, *Recollections*, 93.

92. Payne, *History of the AME Church*, 262.

93. Payne, *Recollections*, 96.

94. Ibid., 99.

95. Ibid., 103.

96. Ibid., 106.

97. *Pittsburgh Press*, 15 March 1953, 16 February 1969; *Carnegie Magazine* (January 1969):21–24; *Pittsburgh Courier* 3 March 1962; *Northside* Chronicle (February 1995): *Pittsburg Post-Gazette* 14 February 1995.

98. Payne, *Recollections*, 106.

99. Ibid.

100. Ibid., 108.

101. Payne, *History of the AME Church*, 271.

102. Payne, *Recollections*, 110.

103. Payne, Ibid.; *History of the AME Church*, 274.

104. Payne, *History of the AME Church*, 276.

105. Ibid., 277.

106. Ibid.

107. *Bishop Payne's First Annual Address to the Philadelphia Annual Conference of the A.M.E.* Church May 16, 1853 (Philadelphia: C. Sherman, 1853).

108. Ibid., 14.

109. Payne, *Recollections*, 115.

110. *Miner Normal School. Institution for the Education of Colored Youth Founded by Miss Myrtilla Miner; Miner Teachers College Catalogue Series I Number 7 Public Schools of the District of Columbia.* Washington, DC 1947–1950.

111. Probate Court Archives Record Search Marriage 1809–1983. Accessed 02–03–2010.

112. Payne, *Recollections*, 123.

113. Sprecher continued on the faculty after his presidency. He was professor of philosophy and theology, 1874–80; professor of systematic theology, 1880–84; and president of the General Synod, 1864–1866. Lutheran Theological Seminary at Gettysburg Archives.

114. Payne, *Recollections*, 116.

115. Payne, *Recollections*, 117.

116. Ibid., 128.

117. Payne, Diary for 1856, Howard University, Moorland-Spingarn Center.

118. Ibid., 1, 2, 3, January; 21, 22 February 1856.

119. Payne, Diary of 1856, 10 December 1856; *Recollections*, 136.

Photograph of Daniel Alexander Payne. Courtesy of the Ohio Historical Society.

Wilberforce University,

(Incorporated in 1863.)

Near Xenia, Greene Co., O. March 30th 1869

Rev. Samuel S. Schmucker D.D.

My Venerable Preceptor

Your kind favor of the 3d, came to hand by due course of mail. It furnished me with just such information as my inexperience needed; for which accept my unfeigned thanks.

But there is one point upon which I had forgotten to ask information, to wit,

a. At what time and place does the President of Pennsylvania College matriculate students, in private at his own studio, or in the presence of the students in the Lecture Room? Another.

b. So far as your knowledge extends, what the general usage?

The Catalogues have also reached. I am thankful for them.

Gratefully Yours

Payne

Letter to the Rev. Samuel S. Schmucker, 30 March 1869. Courtesy of the Lutheran Theological Seminary at Gettysburg, A. R. Wentz Library Seminary Archives, S. S. Schmucker Collection.

MALE AND FEMALE SEMINARY.

RULES.

I. Every scholar shall promise to obey the laws of God.

II. Every scholar shall promise to obey his or her parents or guardians.

III. Every scholar shall promise to obey the teacher of this Seminary.

IV. Every scholar shall endeavor to be in the Seminary before and at morning devotions.

V. Every scholar shall promise to study at home every night before bed-time, and every morning before coming to school.

VI. No scholar shall engage in play or private conversation during the time of study or recitation.

VII. Testimonials of moral character will be required for every child or youth, previously unknown to the teacher. Every ungovernable pupil will be expelled.

VIII. No one except an apprentice will be admitted for a less period than six months.

IX. No scholar will be permitted to use abusive language, or to strike another.

X. No child or youth can be admitted to the membership of this Seminary, until the parent or guardian has promised to maintain a rigid moral discipline at home.

THE PRICES PER QUARTER, FOR

Orthography, Reading, Writing and Arithmetic,	$3 00
Geography, Construction of Maps, English Grammar, Composition, Sacred and Profane History, English and Hebrew Poetry,	5 00
Geometry, Mensuration, Algebra, and Moral Philosophy,	6 00
Physiology, Chemistry, Astronomy, Natural, Intellectual, and Moral Philosophy,	8 00

Greek and Hebrew, extra.

EXPLANATORY REMARKS.

We have introduced the study of Poetry, not with the hope of making poets, but for the purpose of giving a right direction to their literary taste, and an elevated tone to their moral sensibilities. To attain this desirable end, we have selected Cowper, Thomson, Young, Pollock, and Milton; David, Job, and Isaiah. By these instrumentalities, we shall endeavor to inspire them with the sublimest ideas of all that is great and good, in Earth and Heaven.

The more advanced scholars will be taught how to keep the "*Index Rerum.*"

It is with delight I inform the public and my friends that I have obtained the consent of Mr. ROBERT FORTEN to deliver lectures on Astronomy, and give the pupils telescopic views of the heavens, whenever a class can be formed for that purpose.

Ladies and Gentlemen of talents, learning and piety, will be engaged to deliver moral lectures semi-monthly to the pupils; and neither care nor means shall be spared to cultivate their hearts as well as their heads.

With these explanatory remarks we set our Seminary before the public, and commend it to the blessing of that God, in whose wise and benevolent heart are the intellectual and moral interests of the rising generation.

D. A. PAYNE.

REFERENCES.

Mr. ROBERT PURVIS,	Rt. Rev. MORRIS BROWN,
Mrs. HARRIET PURVIS,	Rev. C. W. GARDNER,
Mr. J. J. G. BIAS,	Rev. SOLOMON T. SCOTT,
Mrs. HETTY CREW,	Mr. ELYMUS JOHNSON,
Mr. JOHN A. CHEW,	Mr. GEORGE W. GOINES,
Mr. SAMUEL B. BASS,	Mr. SAMUEL NICKLESS.

Letter to the Rev. Samuel S. Schmucker, 30 March 1869. Courtesy of the Lutheran Theological Seminary at Gettysburg, A. R. Wentz Library Seminary Archives, S. S. Schmucker Collection.

Chapter Three

The Wilberforce Experience: 1856–1876

Immersed in the routines of the bishop's office, in this phase of Payne's life, his call as religious leader and educator coalesced into a dynamic whole. As bishop, Payne continued to be "on the go" he was concerned about and worked tirelessly for his constituency. As an educator he was committed to the education of Black clergymen and laity within the denomination and throughout the United States. The nascent years in South Carolina, theological education at the Lutheran Seminary in Gettysburg, Pennsylvania, and affiliation with the African Methodist Episcopal Church prepared him for the culminating years of his professional life as president of Wilberforce University in Ohio. It was through that experience that he became a national and international leader. Moreover, through his travels in Europe, encountering men and women of the church as well as in government, he cemented his self-identity as religious leader, educator, and a Black intellectual of the nineteenth century. Although these attributes developed and cultivated in the United States, it was in Europe that the three came to full fruition.

THE BISHOP'S WORK CONTINUES

Payne's responsibilities in the initial years as a bishop of the AME Church kept him on the move. These travels took him from friends to his pastoral flock, from congregational and regional meetings to the White House. Payne addressed the local issues as well as the national issues from the lens of the bishop's office. In the midst of this we also see a man very devout in his piety and in the development of his own self-education.

As bishop Payne had responsibility for presiding over the Annual Conferences in his district. On 29 September1856, Payne traveled to and presided over the Annual Conference of the AME Church in Canada for the last time. At this Annual Conference, the Canadian section of the church voted to separate from the American church and became the British Methodist Episcopal Church and Willis Nazrey was elected bishop.[1] It was also determined that the mission-field for the Canadian denomination would be Central America.

In March of 1860 after a long period of travel, on another visit to the Baltimore Conference, Payne accompanied by his colleague Rev. Lynch, booked passage and was assigned a sleeper on the train. However, the thought of a Black man in a sleeping car was apparently abhorrent to a White passenger who contacted the conductor and the porter. They seized Payne and Lynch and forced them into the smoking car. Payne never forgot the words of the Southern man from Tennessee who said, "This is right; we don't allow niggers in our country, in Tennessee, to ride in cars with us white men."[2]

In spite of all the humiliation that took place before arriving in Baltimore, the meeting bore fruit. To this end, Payne noted that on his visit to Bethel Church, he developed the Mental and Moral Improvement Society. This initiative really began with his statements and work on education a decade before; however, he didn't have the clout to influence or enact programs. Payne's interest broadened at this time because he initiated education among the laity with the development of literary and historical organizations in churches. For Payne, "[A]n educated ministry is more highly appreciated by an educated laity, and hence always better supported. They act and react upon each other."[3] As adamant as he was about clergy education, he was equally so in regards to the laity education.

Payne also developed the Mother's Associations in order to counter the effects of slavery with its disruption of family-life. The objective of the Associations was to assist with the raising of children for "the greatest curse which slavery inflicted upon us was the destruction of the home. No home, no mother; no home! But what is home without a cultivated intellect, and what the value of such an intellect without a cultivated heart?"[4]

Payne went on to visit Western Theological Seminary (Presbyterian) in Pittsburgh which indicated his continuing interest in theological education as well as his awareness and appreciation that the institution was open to Black candidates for ministry. He recalled the names of these men whom he encountered. One of them was Benjamin Tanner, a prominent leader of the AME Church who became editor of *A.M.E. Review*, the *Christian Recorder* and later a bishop of the church.[5] One also notes that Tanner had spent his beginning years in higher education at Avery College.

In April 1861, after presiding at the New England Conference, Payne had conversations with the Rev. James Theodore Holly, a black intellectual, of the Protestant Episcopal Church who served as a missionary in Haiti and eventually became Bishop in that denomination. Payne then went to visit Yale and had conversation with Benjamin Silliman, Sr., a science professor at the University.[6] Payne doesn't give us a clue as to his initial acquaintance with Silliman or whether this encounter was his first; however, Payne described his conversation with Silliman in which he solicited Silliman's opinion on slavery. Perhaps Payne sought a scientific point of view of the slavery issue. Whatever the case, Payne described this encounter with these words:

> In conversation I asked him what he considered to be our future—whether slavery would be abolished? He replied: "Yes; I do believe that slavery will be abolished, because there are Christians among them." To me it was a prophecy, as I had never before heard that reason given for the overthrow of that abominable system.[7]

In New York Payne attended a reception for the Episcopal missionary from Liberia, the Rev. Alexander Crummel. It had been 18 years since Payne first encountered Crummel in Philadelphia where he had turned his school over to Crummel following his appointment to oversee Israel AME Church in Washington D.C. in 1843. The Rev. H.H. Garnett[8] who later became the Minister Resident to Liberia was also there. On this trip he also visited with Frederick Douglass, in August, in his home while in Rochester where he marveled at the landscape of his property and delighted in hearing Douglass's daughter, Rosetta, play the piano for what was a culturally stimulating musical evening.

It was during this period of Payne's travels, that upheaval and transformation took place throughout the United States with the outbreak of the Civil War in 1861. Payne's autobiography doesn't identify the beginning of the War, but his words express the turmoil that developed and which he observed during, "the hour of peril…confronting the nation."[9]

In contrast to the unusually balm January in 1862, Payne was in Washington, DC and stated that the capitol of the nation, "looked …more like a great a great military encampment than the seat of national legislation and judicial action. The greatest armies ever seen upon the American continent were preparing themselves for a deadly conflict, and the fate of millions was pendent on the result of their encounters."[10]

Payne noted the irony of the soldiers who were fighting. He could not help but comment, "But the most extraordinary thing of all, and that which forms the greatest anomaly, is the circumstance that the South was earnestly invoking God against the North, the North invoking God against the South, and the blacks invoking God against, both!"[11]

At this time, we see Payne's theological and denominational interests are weaved with the plight of his enslaved brothers and sisters. At the capitol, he saw and talked with politicians: Senator Charles Sumner of Massachusetts,

Rev. Hamilton W. Pierson, president of Cumberland College in Kentucky; Washburn of Illinois was a lawyer, politician, diplomat who was in the House of Representatives from the state if Illinois.[12] He met with Carl Schurz, who had emigrated from Germany and settled in Wisconsin where he was a lawyer and became involved in politics. President Lincoln considered him a good friend and appointed him Minister to Spain.[13] He also met President Abraham Lincoln, himself.

WELCOME THE RANSOMED

In the midst of the War, another issue weighed heavily on the minds of Blacks in the country, and more specifically Blacks in the District of Columbia: the emancipation of Blacks in the nation's capitol. Payne's travels placed him in the District at the time a bill of emancipation in the Capitol was being considered by congress in the spring. The congress passed the bill on April 11, 1862.[14]

The following Sunday 13 April, encouraged by the actions of the congress, Payne preached at Ebenezer A.M.E. Church in Washington. The title of his sermon, "Welcome the Ransomed or Duties of the Colored Inhabitants of the District of Columbia" was based on the scripture text from the First Letter to Timothy, beginning at the second chapter:

> [1]I exhort therefore, that, first of all, supplications, prayers, intercessions, and giving of thanks, be made for all men; [2]For kings, and for all that are in authority; that we may lead a quiet and peaceable life in all godliness and honesty. [3]For this is good and acceptable in the sight of God our Saviour; [4]Who will have all men to be saved, and to come unto the knowledge of the truth.

The clergy who heard the sermon were so impressed by what was said that they asked Payne's permission to have it published and circulated so that all people and especially Black people would benefit from reading it. Payne responded to their request and sent them the manuscript with slight editorial changes in the hope that it might be "productive of good."[15]

The sermon focused on what Payne subtitled the "Redemption of the enslaved people of the District of Columbia." It was the responsibility of each member of the church to welcome them to the boon of freedom. It was also the responsibility of the newly freed to welcome "a well-regulated liberty, sanctioned by the Divine, maintained by the Human law." He called the newly freed to the godly life. Specifically, the passage called on Christians to pray for those in authority through supplications, prayers, intercessions, and thanksgiving. It was God's Spirit which moved the hearts of those lawmakers. Payne, forever the educator, told them as well,

Permit us, also, to advise you to seek every opportunity for the cultivation of your minds. To the adults we say, enter the Sunday Schools and the Night Schools, so opportunely opened by Dr. Pierson, in behalf of the American Tract Society. In these latter you can very soon learn to read the precious word of God, even before you shall have a familiar knowledge of the letters which constitute the alphabet.

Rest not till you have learned to read the Bible. 'Tis the greatest, the best of books. In it is contained the Divine law. O! meditate therein by day and by night, for "the law of the Lord is perfect, converting the soul; the testimony of the Lord is sure, making wise the simple; the statutes of the Lord are right, rejoicing the heart; the commandment of the Lord is pure, enlightening the eyes;—more to be desired are they than gold, yea, than much fine gold; sweeter also than honey and the honeycomb." "In keeping of them there is great reward." Yield uniform, implicit obedience to their teachings. They will purify your hearts and make them the abodes of the Ever-Blessed Trinity.

When you shall have reached this point, you will be morally prepared to recognize and respond to all the relations of civilized and christianized life.[16]

As they would now be getting paid for their jobs, it was necessary for them to obtain, pay for, and give support to the educated teachers and school buildings, for the schoolmasters as well as the preachers. These responsibilities were unitary entities for the betterment of the newly freed.

On the next day, Monday 14 April, Payne was again at the White House visiting with the President. The focus of the conversation which he had with the president was whether Lincoln intended to sign the bill. Again, Payne reported that he was in the company of Washburn and Schurz. President Lincoln met him at the door. Although the issue of signing was paramount in the mind of Payne, Lincoln listened but wouldn't commit himself to say whether or not he would have his signature on the bill. Apparently in the morning, there were those who came to urge him not to do so. Payne's response,

'Mr. President, you will remember that on the eve of your departure from Springfield, Ill., you begged the citizens of the republic to pray for you.' He said, "Yes." Said I: "From that moment we, the colored citizens of the republic, have been praying: 'O Lord just as thou didst cause the throne of David to wax stronger and stronger, while that of Saul should wax weaker and weaker, so we beseech thee cause the power at Washington to grow stronger and stronger, while that at Richmond shall grow weaker and weaker."[17]

Although a commitment was not forthcoming from the Executive Office, Payne left from the White House that evening with "a profound sense of his [President Lincoln's] real greatness and of his fitness to rule a nation composed of almost all the races on the face of the globe."[18] His reflection on Lincoln as a formidable man was in contrast to his memory of his encounter with President John Tyler eighteen years earlier in 1844 when he presided in a parlor of the White House at the funeral of Tyler's slave, Armistead, who died in an explosion on board The Princeton on the Potomac. Tyler was pro-slavery, a son of Virginia.[19] On April 16, President Lincoln signed, "An Act for the Release of certain persons held to serve or labor in the District of Columbia" or The District of Columbia Emancipation Act.[20]

Even with all the upheaval caused by the Civil War and the responsibilities of an ecclesiastical office like Bishop, Payne continued to be focused on education, and this is keenly apparent in his work as trustee and ultimately President of Wilberforce University in Ohio.

PRELUDE TO WILBERFORCE

Although Payne became president of Wilberforce University in 1863, his involvement in this institution of the church began many years before when the idea for the establishment of a university was thought about in the minds of some visionaries of the Methodist Episcopal Church in the preceding decade. One might also say that Payne's life up to this point; his schools in Charleston, South Carolina; his advocacy for an educated ministry in his five essays on education; and his speeches at General and local conferences of the AMEC were prerequisites for his educational leadership at Wilberforce. The culmination of his interest in education came with his presidency of Wilberforce University.

Although Wilberforce University has long been the focal point for identifying the AME Church with education, the church's interest in education can be first documented at the Ohio Annual Conference in 1833 where the following resolution was approved:

> Resolved, 1st. As the sense of this house, that common schools, Sunday schools and temperance societies are of the highest importance to all people, but more especially to our people.

> Resolved, 2d. That it shall be the duty of every member of this Conference to do all in his power to promote and establish these useful institutions among our people.[21]

The next extended discussion on education took place at the Baltimore Conference in 1842 where more specific language and directions were approved in the following resolutions:

Resolved, 1st. That we recommend to all our elders and deacons of the Connection, will from henceforth make use of all the means in our power to cultivate our minds and increase our store of knowledge.

Resolved, 2d. That we recommend to all our elders and deacons, licensed preachers and exhorters, the diligent and indefatigable study of the following branches of useful knowledge, vis.: English grammar, geography, arithmetic, history, modern history, ecclesiastical history, natural and revealed theology.[22]

These resolutions were presented by Payne, and he stated that it was the first strong statement to bring the educational level of the church to "a higher plane of intellectual culture."[23]

Perhaps the most influential event took place in 1845 with the call for the first educational convention by the Baltimore Conference which took place in Philadelphia beginning on 30 October. Representation to the gathering came from the Eastern conferences of Baltimore, Philadelphia, and New York. The convention was spirited, to say the least, with a number of special interests coming to the floor which were divided into three factions. There were those who wanted the establishment of an educational association which would raise funds to educate men for the ministry. Another group wanted the church to establish an institution of higher education in the West.[24] Those who supported the support of funds to send men to be educated for ministry felt that there were already institutions which would accept people of color (Gettysburg Seminary, Oberlin, and Oneida). The group supporting the development of a college felt that the church had enough support to do so. The third faction desired to have a school in the East.[25] At the conclusion of the convention all three interests were approved and each group was to execute its project. Due to lack of unified voices these efforts failed.

In addition to the above efforts, the Ohio Conference formed a committee in 1844 after the General Conference and founded Union Seminary about 14 miles southwest of Columbus. Land was purchased and a modest building erected; however, it didn't succeed as public institutions for children of color were developing in the nearby larger towns and the quality of the education was questionable.[26] The Seminary remained open until the purchase of Wilberforce University by the A.M.E. Church when funds were needed and the property was sold.

In addition to these major educational endeavors, it should also be noted that Rev. Coker also opened a school in the basement of Bethel Church in Baltimore in 1810 Payne could not determine the length of its existence.[27] Furthermore, Payne also established his own grammar school which he opened in Philadelphia in 1840 with support from the Franckean Synod.

While members and leaders of the AME church were concerned about education, their white brothers and sisters were thinking about the educational needs of their Black siblings as well. In Payne's "The History of the Origin and Development of Wilberforce University"[28] he shares the background of the initial impetus for the school which he takes from the documents presented by the Rev. John F. Wright, one of the planners. Wright wrote that the centrality of the Gospel compelled the church to be engaged with all her constituencies. He reported that in 1853 the thinking of some Methodist Episcopal clergy and laity was to make a "concentrated effort to improve the condition and furnish the facilities of education to the thirty thousand colored people in Ohio and those of other free States."[29] At a meeting of the Cincinnati Conference on September 28, 1853, there was a motion that Bishop Janes appoint a committee to investigate the possibility helping the black citizens in their area. Seven members were named to be on the committee and in August, 1854 developed a report which included the following:

1. Resolved, that it is of the greatest importance, both to the colored and white races in the free States, that all the colored people should receive as least a good common school education; and that for this purpose well-qualified teachers are indispensable.
2. That the religious instruction of the colored people is necessary to their elevation as well as their salvation.
3. That we recommend the establishment of a literary institution of high order for the education of the colored people generally, and for the purpose of preparing teachers of all grades to labor in the work of educating the colored people in our country and elsewhere.
4. That we recommend that an attempt be made, on the part of the Methodist Episcopal Church, to co-operate with the African Methodist Episcopal Church in promoting the intellectual and religious improvement of the colored people.
5. That we recommend the appointment of a general agent to carry out the objects proposed in the foregoing resolutions, and to labor otherwise for the improvement of the people of color.
6. That we will furnish all the Conferences in the free States of the West with a copy of our resolutions, and respectfully request them to cooperate with us...[30]

The committee's resolution was shared with other conferences and received positive responses. Subsequently, the committee delivered the report to the Cincinnati Conference on 23 September 1854.

The report is significant in that it indicated the importance of the educational endeavor not only for the benefit of persons of color but for all people in the country; moreover, education was not only to benefit the society within the United States but abroad as well. The resolution also implied that it could not be about this task without the involvement and cooperation of the AME Church. It had to do the work inter-denominationally. The determination to accomplish this project was visible in the focus on identifying a person to act on the church's behalf. In addition to the resolution, the committee added the following: "We give no countenance to any theory which goes to deprive the black man of his full share in our common humanity, but hail him as a man, a brother, in accordance with that grand affirmation of the Bible, which must forever settle the unity of the human race. In that God 'hath made of one blood all nations of men, for to dwell on the face of the earth.'"[31]

It was at this gathering that John F. Wright, a presiding elder, was designated the agent to carry out the resolutions on their behalf. The word must have spread for it is reported that the hopes were ignited among the people in general and the Black constituency in particular.[32]

At the meeting of the Cincinnati Conference held on 28 September 1855, resolutions were adopted. Of particular importance were the following resolutions:

> Resolved, That we recommend the appointment of Rev. John F. Wright as general agent for this Conference, to take the incipient steps for a College for the colored people in this State.
> Resolved, That our delegates be, and are hereby instructed to bring this subject before the next General Conference for their sanction and assistance.
> Resolved, That it be the duty of our general agent to co-operate with the African Methodist Episcopal Churches in promoting Sabbath schools and other educational interests of the colored people.[33]

On 30 April 1856 the legal papers were submitted to the State of Ohio with the corporate name "The Wilberforce University" with a board of 23 members.[34] It was also noted that the submission was in conformity with an Ohio state law that went into effect in 1852 which underscored the corporate nature of establishing educational institutions.[35]

The location of the College was not an issue in that there was land available in Greene County, Ohio at Xenia Springs. The cost of the land was $13, 500 with 6% interest. The offer was good for only 10 days consideration. The Conference representatives brought the matter to the leadership of the General Conference in Indianapolis, Indiana who agreed that the land should be purchased. The report to the General Conference of 22 May 1856 described the view of the property, "It is situated in Greene County, Ohio, very near a good turnpike road, about midway between Cincinnati and Columbus, and near the railway. It is easy of access, and yet retired, in a rural, beautiful and healthy region, and in nearly as mild acclimate as can be obtained north of the Ohio River."[36]

The resolutions that were enthusiastically approved set the priority for offering religious education to the people of color to prepare them to be of use in this country, that the actions on education be attributed to God, and soliciting the prayers and funds from those able to give. Under the conditions of the sale, they had to make a down payment of $3375 by May 24 or the deal would be forfeited. They received the final monies needed thirty minutes before midnight of the 24th of May.

The Rev. Professor F. Merrick was elected the president and Professor James K. Parker was named Principal. The school opened in October 1856 a fact which Payne noted a few years later that this was a school of the church and a place for the elevation of students of color,

> Every year the school has been visited with a gracious revival of religion, and many of the pupils have been made the happy subjects of a work of grace which is deemed all important to their usefulness in life. This benevolent scheme is based on the supposition that the colored man must, for the most part, be the educator and elevator of his own race in this and other lands. Hence, a leading objective of the institution is to educate and thoroughly train many of them for professional teachers, or for any other position or pursuit in life to which God, in His providence, or by his Spirit, may call them.[37]

As a school of the church, it was also important that a theological department become organized to meet the pastoral needs of the church with an educated ministry. This was an important outcome for the organizers of the school.

To take the name of Wilberforce was significant for the developers of a school in the United States. William Wilberforce was an Englishman, states-man, philanthropist, Christian and abolitionist. He was elected to Parliament where he introduced legislation for the elimination of slavery in England. Af-ter many defeats, it was finally passed by the House of Commons on 23 Feb-ruary 1807 which eliminated slave trade and a final emancipation bill which was passed 26 July 1833—Act of Emancipation that eliminated slavery.[38]

The students who attended were students of color. With more probing, it is interesting to see just who these students were. Payne mentioned that when one looked at the enrollment three years after the opening of the school one sees that the majority of the students were the natural children of Southern and Southwestern planters who "came from the plantation with nothing mentally but the ignorance, superstition, and vices which slavery engenders; but departed with so much intellectual and moral culture…"[39] The remaining number of students came from the free States as near as Pennsylvania, Illinois, Ohio, and as far away as California. It was noted from a visitation committee of the Conference reported, two years after its opening, that the school was a success and was thriving: "The examinations showed conclusively that the minds of the present class of students are capable of a very high degree of cultivation."[40] This was certainly against the prevailing notions of the intellectual inferiority of persons of color with the ideology of scientific racism. An examination of the courses in *The Catalogue of the Wilberforce University 1859–60* notes the University was divided into three departments: Collegiate, Academic, and Preparatory. The Preparatory Department provided the students with the requisite studies in order to enter the academic curriculum of the University.[41]

PAYNE'S INVOLVEMENT WITH WILBERFORCE

As previously stated, Payne's involvement with Wilberforce began well before his ascent to the presidency of the university under the AME Church. He, along with three other men of color, was on the board from the beginning years. In fact, Payne was on the Executive Committee of the Board. But his involvement went far beyond the responsibilities of a board member. One recalls that he moved to Tawawa Springs with his family from Cincinnati. He noted that his involvement also included management of the institution as well. He was given this responsibility when the white teachers and management were away at the end of the academic year. In addition, two of Payne's step children were students at Wilberforce.[42] Payne's responsibilities as a board member as well as his daily involvement in the institutional life by being a permanent resident on the campus prepared him for what he had not imagined a few years after Wilberforce's opening, his ascent to the presidency.

From 1856 until June of 1862, Wilberforce was an educational institution of the Methodist Episcopal Church. It was supported by slaveholders in the south who sent their slave offspring there to be educated. However, with the outbreak of the Civil War and the strained economic conditions, southern support ceased. The planters and slaveholders were supportive of the southern cause and withdrew their support. That being the case, the trustees decided to cease operation. On March 10, 1863, Payne noted that he was called to a meeting of the Board of Trustees in Cincinnati which went into the late evening where Payne agreed to purchase the property for the A.M.E. Church.[43] However, Payne was not surprised by the outcome of the board. A few months prior to the March meeting, Payne was told by Dr. Rust that the trustees had decided to sell the property and that the AME Church could secure it for the indebtedness of the institution which was $10,000. Payne began to think of a way of introducing this opportunity to the members of the AME Church. After prayerful consideration, he decided to consult with some of the leading men in the church: Dr. Willis R. Revels, Lewis Woodson, and Stephen Smith. Revels and Woodson were affirmative in attempting to accept the offer. In fact Woodson committed himself to begin a campaign to raise the funds needed. Smith made no comment although Payne noted Smith was the richest man in the church.

Payne attended the March meeting with this background and the trustees strongly urged him to purchase Wilberforce for the A.M.E. church. Payne indicated to them that he needed to consult with the various spring meetings of the Conferences. The Trustees responded with, "Now or never."[44] The reason for an immediate decision on Payne's part was the fact that the State of Ohio informed the trustees that the state was interested in the property in order to establish an asylum.[45] With the State Legislature in session, the elected officials demanded a response from the Wilberforce Board by March 11. Payne took a leap of faith and in the late evening, stated, "In the name of the Lord I buy the property of Wilberforce for the African Methodist Episcopal Church."[46] The response from the Board was, "Amen, amen, amen" and concluded with prayer for the success of Payne's decision. Payne noted that he didn't even have $10 in his pocket "but," he said, "I have faith in God."[47]

The commitment of Payne to this educational enterprise was evident in his letter of appeal to the AME Church membership which was published in *The Christian Recorder*. He commented on his move and the move of Rev. James Shorter to the institution to educate their families as early as 1856 and 1857 respectively to educate their children. He affirmed their decision by stating, "it has done us good, and nothing but good."[48] In a letter to the Editor the two months later, support came from a William H. Longfellow who was writing against the colonizationists supporting the return of Blacks to Africa but adds in his closing comments the following:

A word about another matter and I will close; Bishop Payne is engaged in an enterprise that appears to me would reflect more credit upon the colored people, and bring down more blessing from Heaven, than all the African Colonization Societies have done since their organization; that is, the purchasing of Wilberforce College and lands. That, sir, if accomplished, will speak louder than thunder, and will shine as bright as the noon-day sun, and generations unborn will exclaim, God bless Daniel A. Payne and others who may be interested in securing it! Yes, sir, when the ink shall have grown pale that with the history of Bishop Payne and when the winds and rain shall have erased off the letter that may have been engraved on his marble tomb, this college and land will be a living witness of his worth and virtues.[49]

The commitment by Payne and other members of the AME Church for the acquisition of Wilberforce was further demonstrated by the fact that by June of that year, just three months after making a verbal commitment to purchase the University, the Church was able to meet its first payment of $2500. Illustrative of this commitment is a letter of ecclesial and personal appeal from Payne himself in the church's magazine,

> Nature seems to have designed it for a place of study, meditation, intellectual, moral and religious training. The marvellous providence of God has placed this splendid property with all its assets into my hands, and through me into the hands of the colored race, to be used for the benefit of all races. Feeling the pressure of this great responsibility, like a load forcing me into the grave, I call upon the ministry, laity, and friends of the African M.E. Church, and ask them if they will respond to the voice of God, and pay for this property? The trustees have given every guarantee that can be reasonably asked. I have a written article, that just as soon as we will pay them $3,000, a quit claim deed will be made out, conveying the whole into the hands of trustees appointed by our church. In addition to this, they have given up the management of the property and school into my hands, as the representative of the said church. But this first installment must be paid within three months, dating from the 10th of March, which was the day when I assumed the responsibility.[50]

Enthusiasm for the educational commitment must have been high as within two years of that initial payment, the church was able to pay the $7, 500 balance owed.

WILBERFORCE UNIVERSITY AND THE A.M.E. CHURCH

On June 11, 1863, the deed for Wilberforce University was transferred to the A.M.E. Church into the hands of the Rev. James A. Shorter, Professor John G. Mitchell, and Bishop Daniel A. Payne who were the church's representatives. With the new incorporation, a new board of trustees was elected. In addition, Daniel Payne was elected president with only one negative vote which was cast by Rev. Shorter.[51] With that vote Payne became the first African American to be president of an institution of higher education in the United States. This was an accomplishment for the AME Church as well as a monumental accomplishment for Black people within the United States most of whom were still in the bonds of slavery.

Although he had responsibilities as chief administrative officer for Wilberforce, Payne was still a bishop of the church. These duties were indicative of

Payne's two vocational loves: love for the church and passion for education. He expressed these double-duty responsibilities when he wrote,

> In this manner I began my connection with Wilberforce University as its President—a connection that lasted for thirteen years, and in which I assumed the double duties of head of an infant institution and one of the heads of the whole Church. My work henceforth was to lie in two channels, and my whole heart, soul, and body were to need strength from on high to wisely perform it.[52]

The following months Payne highlighted his ecclesial travels. He visited and described the scene of some 500 Black children in a Norfolk, Virginia Sunday school being taught by teachers from northern states. A new day was dawning before his eyes and before and within the eyes of these former slaves. He wrote, "The contrast which this scene made with the previous state of things made me feel that the reign of slavery, darkness, and cruelty was passing away, and that of freedom, light, mercy, and love was dawning upon an outcast, outlawed, enslaved race!"[53]

In addition, he and the other two clergy, A. W. Wayman and J.M. Brown visited the black soldiers of the First Regiment in Virginia as well. In addition, he received a letter of introduction from James Barnes, the military governor in order to meet with military personnel in Mississippi. He also was on hand to organize two congregations in Nashville, whereupon, he met with Governor Andrew Johnson who offered him assistance as he went about his ecclesial responsibilities. Ever the traveler, he ventured east of Nashville to the home of General Andrew Jackson, the Hermitage.

At the General Conference held in Philadelphia which convened on 2 May 1864, Payne was recommended to the people of Great Britain to be the representative of the AME Church as its agent. At the same meeting, Wilberforce was officially established as the property of the AME Church. Steps were also taken at the Conference to form a connection with the AME Zion Church which would be ratified by both denominations at the 1868 General Conference of each. However, the business at the meeting was cut short and concluded with news that the confederate army was retreating due to pursuit by the Army of the Potomac.[54] The following July, Payne was in New York speaking with officials of the American Missionary Association attempting to establish a school for girls in Baltimore. He also visited with the National Freedman's Relief Association in order to make arrangements to send missionaries to South Carolina.[55] The travel must have taken a toll on Payne because he was forced to stay in New York for the reason that he fell ill and was unable to attend the Board of Trustees meeting or the first graduation at Wilberforce under the AME Church. After recuperating for about ten days, he was able to return to Wilberforce and take on the challenges of the presidency.

In April of 1865 Payne was again in Baltimore for the Annual Conference. It was at the conference on the fourteenth of the month that news reached the delegates that President Lincoln was assassinated. The emotions upon the tragic loss of the nation's president ran very high among the delegates at the meeting with members expressing aloud their feelings.[56] Immediately, resolutions were written and passed by the conference delegates. However, that was not the only tragic news that took place that day. Payne received word that the central building at Wilberforce burned. The recitation rooms, housing for teachers and students, kitchen, laundry and chapel were there. When Payne returned to the campus in June, he recalled his sentiments, "...as I stood and gazed on the ruins my heart ached, but my spirit soared to heaven, and as my faith laid hands upon the strong arm of the Almighty I said, "From these ashes a nobler building shall arise!"[57] Indeed, his confidence and faith extended throughout the denomination. Appeals for the rebuilding of the edifice were publicized throughout the church in the subsequent months, with support coming from churches as well as fraternal organizations.[58]

At the end of the month, Payne served as one of the Life Directors of The Colored People's National Monument which was organized 25 April in Washington, DC to the memory of President Lincoln. In a letter of appeal for funds they savored the memory of this president for they felt, "in no other way can the people of color so well perpetuate the memory of Abraham Lincoln, as by carrying out, in this manner, the great aim he had in view—the education of their race throughout the land.—this Association confidently relies upon the hearty co-operation of all true friends of the venerated dead. Churches, Sabbath schools, Masonic and Odd Fellows' societies, Benevolent and all other associations, especially of colored persons, every where, and regiments, officers and soldiers, all are most earnestly called upon to contribute to aid of this work."[59]

A month later, in May, Payne finalized his plans for a return to South Carolina, as the church was working on its missionary endeavors with the American Missionary Association which had given some subsidy for that work. He departed on the steamship "Arago" along with the designated missionaries, James A. Hardy, an elder as well as James H. A. Johnson and T.G. Steward.[60] It had been thirty years since Payne had left South Carolina after passage of racist legislation. Upon seeing the first glimpse of the state from the boat, Payne remarks, "The first sight of my native State was followed by indescribable feelings, that of my native city by pleasurable and sad emotions rapidly interchanging, and the passage through the city was attended by the same." He goes on to state, "Yes, after thirty years to the day and the hour when the spirit of slavery forced me away from my native city, Charleston, S. C., I returned, led by the triumphant genius of freedom."[61] An editorial on the event added to the importance and change that had occurred in the city of Payne's birth, with the end of the Civil War, "The fall of this city opened the way for the return of Joseph, in the person of Bishop Daniel A. Payne, to his brethren, he having been made ruler over all the Church in the land of Abraham. He returns to establish Zion in his native city."[62] The South Carolina Conference opened on 15 May with the ordination of deacons and the following Sunday, Payne preached at Trinity Church upon the ordination of two Elders.

Again the hectic pace to accomplish all that he could on the trip led him to preach at a Presbyterian Church and at a Methodist Episcopal church. He went on to visit and observe the education of former slaves being taught by white teachers from the north in various schools. The scenes, however exciting to see, were emotionally draining. Thirty years had indeed changed the atmosphere. In the midst of bullet holes and charred buildings, the sight of those students who only a short time ago were denied the privilege of an education because the hue of their skin, signaled a new day indeed.

Further work in that spring of 1865 included attending the South Carolina Annual Conference, visiting schools in Hilton Head, Beaufort and other schools on the coast of South Carolina as well as Savannah, Georgia where most of the teachers were from the northern states.

The glimpse at his travels gives us a view of the Reconstruction period. From the end of the Civil War to the beginning of the Twentieth Century, the United States was rebuilding its social, economic, and political life. The outbreak and subsequent war brought the national growth to a standstill.[63] The freeing of four million slaves had a impact on the nation. At the same time the influx of immigrants from other parts of the world compounded the social change occurring. As one focuses on the black experience during this time, one notes the way in which Blacks sought to gain as much independence as possible.[64] Church life and practices grew in importance as the striving for education. It is no wonder that various levels of radical changes during this period made life very fragile. Payne notes the instability and danger:

> In conversations which I had already held with several in authority while in the South, it was their plainly-expressed opinion that unless military commanders of a decided and uncompromising anti-slavery character were sent to control the South for several years, the condition of the freedmen would be a deplorable one—little better, if not worse, than slaves. What did follow the plan of reconstruction we well know.[65]

In the midst of this Reconstruction at Wilberforce, Payne undertook a concerted effort in 1866 to raise funds for the university and encountered a variety of responses from those encounters: encouragement from notables as

Wendell Phillips the abolitionist,[66] financial contributions from others like Chief Justice Chase who had been appointed by President Lincoln and from whom he received $250, but discouragement or suspicion from others, as when he spoke to a Pastors' Association in New York and they gave nothing. Nevertheless, Payne was committed to the task. In addition to his fund-raising efforts, in April, he completed *The Semi-Centenary and the Retrospection of the African Meth. Episcopal Church in the United States of America.*[67] It was commissioned by Payne's fellow A.M.E. bishops. Payne wrote that the request was made on January 10 and the book was completed two months later in March. The text, an apologetic of the A.M.E. Church, served more importantly to show the perseverance of those people of color, who despite the odds established a denomination in the midst of overt oppression within the country and within Methodism itself. As Payne stated in the preface: "Its design is to show what that humble band, without learning, without wealth, without prestige, and, therefore, friendless, has done in the brief period of fifty years; and that it has done all this, with not other means than patient labor, self-denial and faith in God."[68]

The Dedication is interesting in that Payne dedicates his book to his seminary classmates at Gettysburg.

> To you Gentlemen, I dedicate this little book, the first product of my literary labors, which is like to attract the notice of Philanthropists and Christians…
>
> I dedicate this book, to you Gentlemen, whom I regard as my greatest earthly benefactors, not so much on account of the food, raiment and home which you furnished me, as on account of the culture you gave me, while I was a student at Gettysburg—you yourselves being my fellow students![69]

Some twenty-nine years after leaving the seminary, he identifies by name his classmates who were members in the "Society of Inquiry on Missions" to which Payne was a member. The book is divided into two parts, The first concerned with Methodism among the English and the white Methodists on American soil with such entries as "Does Methodism Degrade the Anglo-Saxon," "Definition of Methodism," "Methodism among the Anglo-Americans," "Educational Institutions Planted by Methodism." The second part, the majority of the text focuses, on Methodism and its attraction to African Americans. Although theologically trained in the Lutheran theological tradition, Payne is committed to the Methodism. Some of the section titles include: "Does Methodism Degrade the Negro?" "Origin of Methodism among the Anglo-Africans," "Its Persecution in Charleston." The emphasis of the author can be noted by the following entries: "First Action on Education by Ohio Annual Conference," First Action of New York on Education," "The Philadelphia Conference on Education," "First Open Collision between

Ignorance and Education, occurred in Baltimore," "First Regular System of Studies for the Ministry of the A.M.E. Church," "First Educational Convention," "An Educated Ministry" testify to Payne's clear emphasis. In a sense, this last entry is a subtext of the entire book. The concluding words express it best, "Make the African Methodist Episcopal Church a Temple before whose altars all men, without respect to rank, race, or color, shall stand as equals; knowing no difference but that which angels know—the difference created by superior knowledge, superior love, superior holiness."[70]

Following the publication of the history, Payne was instrumental in organizing and participating in the Semi-Centenary celebrations in the spring and fall respectively. At the January 1866 Pittsburg meeting of the bishops, they agreed to emphasize this accomplishment with the following plans:

1 The first Sabbath in March the preparatory services shall be held in each and every church throughout the bounds of our Connection, to consist of preaching and special prayer to the great Head of the Church for his blessing upon the Semi-Centenary services, at which time the pastors shall read the address of the bishops to the churches.

2 The Semi-Centenary services shall be held in all of our churches and places of worship throughout the entire Connection, on Sabbaths 8th and 15th, and Monday 16th of April next, to consist of historical sermons by the pastors, or some one appointed by them, in which they shall review the doings of God toward us as a Christian denomination during the last half century.

3 The Sunday school superintendents and teachers throughout the Connection shall unite in those services in their several schools, in the way they may think best, or as the Central Committee, hereafter appointed for the several Annual Conferences, may direct.

4 At each service; held April next, by both churches and Sunday schools, special collections shall be raised for the following objects: missions, education, Book Concern, and the Superannuated Preachers' Fund, to be divided as follows: one third for Wilberforce College, one third for the missionary cause, and one third to be equally divided between the Book Concern and the Superannuated Preachers' Fund of each Annual Conference.

5 The part for education shall be returned to the Annual Conferences by the pastor and shall be paid by the Conferences to the agent or agents of Wilberforce College. The part for missions shall be returned to the Annual Conferences and applied to the missionaries in their bounds (if any), and should there be none, the money shall be sent to James H. Davis, treasurer of the Parent Missionary Society, Baltimore, Maryland. The part for the Book Concern and Superannuated Preachers' Fund shall also be returned to the Annual Conferences, and

there divided, one half to be paid over to the treasurer, Rev. Stephen Smith, of Philadelphia, Pa., and his receipt taken for the same; the remaining half to be at the disposal of the Annual Conferences.

6 As the Methodist Episcopal Church has extended an invitation to all the members of the great Methodist family to join in the celebration of the Centenary of Methodism in America, we cordially accept said invitation, and shall celebrate it in our churches in October next, at which time the collections will be renewed and applied as above stated.

The festivities culminated at Wilberforce University on October 31, 1866, with a celebration that established the College Aid Society to support indigent students.[71]

PAYNE ABROAD

If there is theme for the beginning and duration of the year1867, the theme would be fund-raising. Payne's days were centered on raising funds for the operation of Wilberforce. While much of this was the responsibility of the president, there were also other interested persons concerned with helping with the awesome task. At the beginning of the year a request came to ask the influential women in the South to raise money for the institution. The Board authorized Payne "to select and empower such ladies as he in his judgment thinks worthy to do something toward raising monies to assist Wilberforce."[72] To this end, the board also authorized Payne to go to England for the purpose of raising funds. In order for this to be accomplished, the board also directed the Board secretary to correspond with certain women in the Baltimore, Washington, and Norfolk areas to make them aware of this effort and to suggest that they organize some ways to monetarily support Payne on this venture.[73]

To gain additional funds, Payne made personal visits to various individuals and organizations for support such as the Unitarian ministers and Dr. Childs of the Depository of the American Tract Society. He also secured letters of introduction from William Lloyd Garrison, Chief Justice Chase, and other influential persons.[74] During his absence, the Rev. A. W. Wayman was designated interim president of Wilberforce.

Having secured the financial support to venture abroad, Payne applied and received his passport on 29 April 1867[75] and on 8 May 1867, Payne boarded the steamship "Cuba" in New York bound for Europe. Payne was not alone during this trip for he encountered familiar faces. On board were William Lloyd Garrison, as well as George Thompson, the English anti-Slavery lecturer.[76] After a pleasant and uneventful sail, unlike his 1846 voyage, the ship arrived in Liver-pool, England on 18 May; from there Payne traveled to London.

Payne's time in London proved to be productive. Similar to his activities in the United States, Payne was a person on the move. In addition to his primary purpose for the trip, to procure money for Wilberforce University, Payne worshipped and preached in various Protestant churches, spoke to various groups about the race issue in the United States, visited places of interest as the interested tourist.

Daniel Payne was foremost a clergyman and representative of his church. One must note that there was an ecumenical spirit in his worship life. While in London he commented on the worship at the Queen Street British Wes-leyan Methodist Church. There, the liturgy reminded him of the Anglican Church worship experience. It was difficult for him to imagine that he was in a Methodist Church until he heard the sermon. He commented:

> It was not until the pastor ascended the pulpit, without a gown of any kind, and entered into an extemporaneous prayer having all the warmth, compass, and power of a true Methodist that I perceived I was really in such a Church. As the pastor became eloquent and enthusiastic, gathering into his arms and offering to the throne of God all nations and Christians of all the earth, my own soul melted and flowed into my eyes; for I thought of my own flock and my own native land, which needed the continual smiles of the Eternal upon them.[77]

The Methodist Payne relishes the moment. During that same Sunday, in the afternoon, Payne attended worship at St. Paul's Cathedral where he heard Canon Melville, a seasoned homiletician, deliver the sermon. In comparing the two sermon experiences, Payne commented,

> The style differed widely from that of the one heard in the morning, being characterized by more of logic and less of rhetoric; more of the sober, of the common life of Christianity, and less of the beauties of the imagination. This difference might be the result rather of age and experience than of brain and mental training; for the Methodist preacher was a very young man, and therefore ardent, while Canon Melville was an old man, and therefore dealt more with the stern realities of the Christian pilgrimage.[78]

He also heard Charles Spurgeon the noted preacher[79] at the English Baptist Church and he listened to the noted theologian Arthur Penrhyn Stanley[80] at Westminster Abbey. Almost an aside, Payne noted that there he "was awe-struck, and seemed to be moving among the dead." It was there that he "paused" in front of the statue of Wilberforce, whose figure was not as he imagined. The statue at the university depicted Wilberforce as a young man, the figure before Payne represented Wilberforce in his waning years.[81]

In addition to the worship services, Payne was able to attend special meetings of the Methodist Church, like the Mission House of the Wesleyan Methodists where Payne received his first donation; and special interest groups like the British Methodist deliberations at which time he was called upon to speak about Methodism among the people of color in the United States; the Aboriginal Protection Society, a human rights organization; the Midnight Meeting Movement which assisted in caring for and reforming female prostitutes;[82] and the Band of Hope which was a temperance society for working-class children.[83] Moreover, the need to share the Word of God meant that he also had the opportunities to preach and speak on the status of Wilberforce University and the people of color within the denomination in the United States. His deliberations with the above specialized groups, enabled him to meet with individuals in the area covering a broad social spectrum; from an Alexander McArthur, a millionaire and Charles Francis Adams, the United States ambassador to England, to the Rev. and Mrs. Tucker. In a spirit of ecumenism, Tucker invited Payne to make a financial appeal to members of his Baptist church.[84]

Another part of Payne's travel in Europe centered on his own cultural adventures; that is, Payne was also a typical nineteenth century American tourist in England. He took in the laying of the corner-stone of Memorial Hall of Art and Science or Royal Albert Hall in memory of Prince Albert. He stated, "We stationed ourselves, with others, in Hyde Park, at the gate-way through which the queen must pass, where we had a full view of her noble face as she rode past with her two daughters."[85]

Payne was particularly struck by the materials in the British Museum. Here we see his interest in ancient civilizations and culture. Payne wrote,

I paid frequent visits to the British Museum, where I was especially interested in the antiquarian department, where the fragmentary monuments of the civilization and greatness of those four nation—Greece, Rome, Assyria, and Egypt—which each in turn controlled the destinies of the world, so far as human agency can control human destiny. These antiquities are very serviceable in two ways—to show how powerful and intelligent a people may become, and how evanescent is all their glory. O may modern nations be rendered wise by their study! In collecting and preserving these antiquities England has done immense service to mankind.[86]

Payne also was a frequent visitor to the Royal Academy of Arts. Here one observes Payne's artistic interests. While he mentions the sculptures and engravings, he identified the historical pictures including, "Last Hours of Cromwell," "Last Sunday of Charles the Second," and "Bondage of the Israelites in Egypt." In addition, Payne, always a lover of books and reading, was struck by the circular reading-room which, in his opinion, had no rival in the United States.[87]

The tourist Payne paid a visit to Windsor Castle which he described as "a majestic pile of buildings on the brow of a towering hill. The most remarkable feature of this stupendous castle is the several other towers. From this tower the standard of Great Britain floats whenever the sovereign is present. From this tower we had a fine view of twelve counties, which were identified by the guide, himself one of the royal guards."[88] Payne seems to be taking it all in with a passion.

One assumes that Payne ventured on his own or within a group. There were times when he was with friends. One example is the time spent with George Thompson when the gentleman called on Payne at the boarding house and invited him to see some of the sights of the city. Payne mentions going to Covent Garden Market, Army and Navy Department, the chief political club-houses, the ancient palace of Charles II, Westminster Hall, the House of Commons and the House of Lords.[89]

Yet the main focus continued to be on collecting funds for Wilberforce University. Payne attempted on two occasions to visit the secretaries of the Evangelical Alliance while in London; however, both persons were out of the office, one in Berlin and the other in Paris. On a third visit, Dr. Herman Schmetteau, one of the secretaries of the Alliance, suggested that Payne attend the meeting of the Evangelical Alliance which would be held in August in Amsterdam. There he would surely encounter a number of benevolent individuals who would be open to hearing his requests.

Payne also connected with other groups while in London. One meeting which apparently made an impression on European clergy took place in Bristol with the Wesleyan Methodists. On 25 July 1867 the opening of the 124th meeting of the English Methodists began. Emile Cook, a French Methodist clergyman was a representative and presenter to the conference, in a three- part series in *L'Evangeliste*,[90] described the pre-conference events, personalities, and issues which took place. With over 600 delegates in attendance, Cook identified Payne along with other international guests from Ireland, Australia, Canada, and France. Payne noted his own presence there where he "…was received as a brother by nature and a brother by grace."[91] His interest centered on some of the deliberations which included the administration of missions and educational institutions and issues of clergy discipline. He also witnessed the ordination of sixty men into the ministry. Payne addressed the meeting twice on the state of Methodism within the United States. His address to the Committee on Foreign Missions on that Wednesday 24 July was reported by M. Jaulmes, editor of *L'Evangeliste*, who described Payne in the following words:

> ….Moreover a large number of pastors and laity who took part in the discussion which followed the reading of the reports, one heard Bishop Payne of the African Methodist Church. With a strong black complexion, slim built, quick intellect,

dignified deportment, Bishop Payne speaks with remarkable facility and purity. It was 51 years ago he said, last April 16 (slavery had then reached, in the United States, the height of its power), that the African Methodist Episcopal Church was born in the city of Philadelphia. She counted only 5000 members, 7 itinerant preachers, and included Bishop Allen, who was the first bishop. The first four bishops were men with limited education; they had only two places of worship. At the end of the first decade, the number of pastors were only 17, and the total sum for their upkeep didn't amount to more than 1500 dollars, 7,500 francs. They had to combat against their own weakness and against what one calls in the United States, Negrophobia, that is to say from the most gigantic system of oppression that the world has known, and that Wesley calls with reason "the awful sum of all depraved acts." But despite these terrible obstacles, African Methodism, at the end of the 50 first years, that is to say, in 16 April 1866, found itself to have by the preaching of the Gospel, so developed the human feelings of this degraded race, that the transformation was complete. Here moreover, what were the results obtained before emancipation: chapels, 286; pastors, 185; annual conferences, 10; circuits, 39; missionaries, 40; students and instructors in the Sunday school; members of the church, 50,000; volumes in the libraries, 17,818. The value of the properties of the church was 825,000 dollars; which is 4,100,000 French francs. Moreover, the churches collected, during the year that preceded the abolition of slavery, 500,000 francs to support their pastors, by their missions and their other general works, without counting the 15,000 francs for Sunday schools, and 25,000 francs for widows and orphans. As fruits of the 50 years of work, these churches have founded: a missionary society for internal, a society for foreign missions, 40 missionary societies that attach themselves ten annual conferences; an equal number of societies to come to the aid of ill pastors or widows of pastors; 6 education societies, 5 literary associations, a library and a periodical journal entitled the Christian Record. They have, moreover, founded a theological institution, having all the characteristics of a university, and to which one gave the name Wilberforce University. But since emancipation, progress has been more rapid. That which filled at first an inexplicable joy, is that slavery received a death blow. We are free as the air; we are no longer contraband material; we are no longer released men, but free people. As the ballot box is sovereign, one now sees the governors who were formerly too proud in regard to the poor negro, to tip their hats. And you see what has been for our church, the glorious results of these first years of liberty. We have four more annual conferences than we had in 1866; the number of our churches amounts to 673, our preachers amount to 509, our stations amount to 110, our mission amount to our members total 130, 950, that is to say 80, 950 more than in 1866. The Sunday schools progressed proportionally, as well as the students who attend them. The number of our chapels, their material worth, the gifts and collections for the various branches of the church; all increased in proportion fills us with and recognition toward God....G Jaulmes[92]

Payne must have left a powerful impression in his report for his presentation is mentioned subsequent editions of the newspaper.[93]

In the following edition of the newspaper, one notes another editorial comment on the meeting and on Daniel A. Payne:

> One heard equally in this session, and with great interest, a bishop of color, the
> Rev. Dr. Payne (1), a member of the African Methodist Church in the United
> States.(1) We reproduced, in our last edition, a part of the discussion which he
> delivered before the Committee on Missions Abroad.[94]

These newspaper articles are significant in examining Payne's venture
abroad. Payne is accepted as an African American Bishop representing the
African Methodist Episcopal Church. In the same manner, he is accepted for
his intellect and his presentation to the clergy group. With his presentation
cited in two editions of the newspaper, there was the indication of the importance of and positive impression of his presentation to the group.

Payne continued to visit a number of prominent persons in the London before he continued on to the next phase of this European travels. One gathering
of note found Payne at St. James Hall where there was a luncheon in honor
of William Lloyd Garrison who had been on the same ship as Payne coming
to Europe. Payne recalled the presence of John Bright who was a Member
of Parliament, a strong advocate for the preservation of the American Union,
and of John Stuart Mill, the philosopher and statesman. In response to their
speeches and those of others, Garrison shared his views on the abolitionist
movement in the United States.[95]

Up to the time that he departed for Amsterdam, Payne continued to visit
and preach in congregations in the area as well as making personal visits to
individuals. On 18 August he departed by steamer for Amsterdam. Upon
arriving, he and others attending the meeting were greeted at the station by
a welcoming committee. After presenting his carte de visite, Payne was directed to the Hoyeler family who would be his host during his stay. Payne
described the family as "...Christian people whom I shall remember with
respect, gratitude, and love as long as memory lasts, because of their genial
hospitality and many special acts of kindness, which endeared them to my
soul."[96] That evening they took him to worship at the French Wallon Church.
The following day, some members of the family accompanied him to the
opening service of the Evangelical Alliance which took place at New Church
and incorporated the Dutch, English, German and French languages and
included Scriptures, hymnody, and prayers. There were about 4000 people
present where the Rev. Dr. Van Oosterizee preached.[97]

The meeting of the Evangelical Alliance from the eighteenth through the
twenty-eighth of August allowed Payne to listen to and encounter some of the
most prominent theologians of the time. One gets the sense of the diversity
and global flavor of this encounter when he recalled some of the speakers

and topics for the week. Payne described the papers which were presented as "interesting, elaborate, and valuable in an historic sense." Payne mentioned the presence of Dr. McCosh who at the time of the conference was a professor at Belfast College in Ireland who would eventually become President of Princeton University. His paper was entitled "Moral Philosophy in Relation to Theology;" Dr. Edward Steane of London, spoke on "Religious Liberty;" and Dr. Eugen Bersier of Paris "Independent Morality."[98] Payne noted that the format was formidable; however, his frustration came from the fact that he had limited or no ability in Dutch, German or French. Although Payne found the sessions interesting, he also noted that some commented on the bland nature of the discussions, particularly at the beginning when the temperature was very warm and the vast and general scope of the papers, i.e. the state of religion in various parts of the world.[99] However, the state of religion in the United States as well as the situation in post-Civil War United States stirred the most interest to the delegates.

The report of Henry Boynton Smith, professor at Union Theological Seminary and chairman of the Executive Committee of the United States branch of the Evangelical Alliance, indicated that there were a growing number of Baptists and Methodists in the country where there were 54,000 places of worship.[100] For all these churches, places of worship, the emancipation of four million former Black slaves brought enormous work. There was a great need to instruct as well as to evangelize the recently freed population. The report also mentioned a number of the agencies that were formed in order to help with this work including the government sponsored Freedman's Bureau, the American Missionary Association, and the American Freedman's Union Commission.

At the missionary meeting Payne addressed the members of the conference on missions within the AME Church; however, he spoke for only fifteen minutes, not that he didn't have more to say but that was the time allotted to English speakers in attendance. Fifteen minutes while those who spoke in Dutch spoke for thirty minutes, Payne complained.[101]

Payne's reflections on attending the meeting of the Evangelical Alliance characterize the highlight of this ecumenical encounter. He stated, "Intellectually I was benefitted, for I learned much of men and things which were new to me."[102] In addition, his personal encounters with men and women of culture and theological scholars of note provided some measure of comfort beyond cursory hearing of their papers.

After the meeting of the Evangelical Alliance, Payne ventured to France for the first of several visits for a meeting of the Anti-slavery Conference in Paris 26–27 August 1867 at the Salle Herz where Edward Laboulaye, lawyer and author, presided.[103] Although he attended the meeting, Payne also attempted to raise sympathetic concerns to the financial needs of Wilberforce.

He did not have success on that phase of his trip.[104] We do get a flavor of his work there as his speech was reproduced in the proceedings of the meeting. Payne addressed the meeting at the end of the first day. Laboulaye introduced him "as a representative of the despised and humble, but equally noble band of Christians, known as the African Methodist Episcopal Church in the United States of America." He underscored the fact that although unlettered, the slaves were cognizant of the Gospel which invited all people; a God who saved all people, whose houses of worship were for all. Payne gave a brief history of the church's development as well as statistics of its various ministries. He concluded with a rhetorical flourish: "and you will see that in *some things* we have quadrupled ourselves, in *others* we *doubled* ourselves, in *all things* we have *improved* ourselves. Our movements have not been backward, but forwards; not downwards, but upwards; not towards death, but towards life."[105]

From Payne's initial stay in France, as well as his own declaration and depiction of his times there, France and specifically Paris emerges as the culmination of his European tour. While he enjoys and takes in similar cultural experiences as he had in England, it is in Paris, that in addition to being the tourist, Payne not only preached in congregations, spoke on behalf of Wilberforce University, but also attended lectures, studied the French language, complemented and completed his own self-education.

Payne's second trip to Paris began on the 30th of September when he participated in a worship service at the request of the Rev. Emile Cook by assisting with the Eucharist. Cook, a French Methodist, was pastor of Wesleyan Congregation Church.[106] In this setting, Payne encountered and commented on the difficulty and strenuousness of the art and skill of; translation. He stayed in Paris for one month, but, does not account for his time. Nevertheless, one might venture to guess that the visit included more of the same: encountering church leaders and presenting the work of Wilberforce University to philanthropic organizations.[107]

Payne's third and most extensive period in Paris lasted five months beginning in November of 1867. Upon correspondence from Payne and their own deliberations, the Board of trustees of Wilberforce University acknowledged Payne's difficulty in raising funds for the institution. In a board action at the October meeting, the board agreed to support Payne financially in order for him to make an extensive survey of the funding sources. In January of 1868 in an emergency meeting of the Board approved the borrowing of additional funds to assist Payne in staying in Europe.[108] It appeared that Payne was very deliberate in telling the story of Wilberforce to any who were willing to listen. In correspondence to the interim President Weyland, Payne requested that the secretary of the Board send 100 Wilberforce catalogues.[109]

It was during this portion of his European pilgrimage that while he continued to be an ambassador for Wilberforce, we find Payne expanding his intellectual pursuits and continuing to be the typical American tourist of his day. Payne was visibly struck by the beauty of France's landscape. As he traveled from Rouen to Paris he could only remark, "La France est un bel pays" (France is a beautiful country).[110]

An examination of Payne's educational pursuits indicates that he was a serious student of French culture, life and literature. He perfected his facility with the language by securing a tutor who spent a portion of each day with Payne in the study of the French language. Payne's facility with the language must have improved because he admits to reading a number of French scientific, literary, and theological works.[111]

Payne's passion for the intellectual life in Paris was reinforced by attending lectures at the Sorbonne[112] and the College de France.[113] Within the gates of these renowned institutions, Payne listened to presentations by eminent Protestant and Roman Catholic scholars of the day. He commented on hearing Ernst Renan, the author of *La Vie de Jesus* (The Life of Jesus); and Dr. Edmond De Pressensé, the French Protestant theologian, preacher and politician.[114]

Payne also attended the lectures of and had personal contact with Professor Edward Laboulaye who had presided at the Antislavery meeting in Paris.[115] The lectures were based on Montesquieu's *Spirit of Laws* which, while not the most stimulating in content, Payne noted, were made interesting by Laboulaye's brilliant illustrations and his witticisms.[116] In addition to Laboulaye, Payne became acquainted with Prof. Jean Louis Armand de Quatrefages,[117] an ethnologist and naturalist whom Payne described as unequaled in his research; Dr. Eugène Casalis,[118] president of the House of Mission and Louis Lysius Salomon, the minister from Haiti whom Payne described as "not only un homme grand, but as I have been told, un grand homme." Solomon went on to serve as the president of Haiti from 1878–1888.[119]

In addition to encountering the intelligentsia and savants of the day, Payne observed French education. He noted visiting a private Protestant boarding school under the directorship of Mlles. Hooper and [Creisseil] Cresseil.[120] The *Paris Protestant* contains an outline of the curriculum of the school operated by a Madame Gay-Creisseil, outside of Paris in Neuilly-sur-Seine: The courses included piano, sight-singing, literature, mathematics, German, natural science. The tuition was 1,200 to 1,500 francs for French students and 1,500 to 2,000 francs for foreign students.[121] This school was established to educate English and French Protestant young ladies. Payne commented on the method of instruction in a natural history course; oral instruction was the pattern. Despite the apparent freedom for students, Payne also observed the behavior which was displayed by the students. This school was operated by a

committee consisting of two of the prominent religious leaders of nineteenth
century French Protestantism, Eugène Bersier and Edmond de Pressensé.[122]
Both of these men had also attended the meeting of the Evangelical Alliance
in Amsterdam. The school's objective was to assist in complementing the
education of young women from French families of Paris with moral and
Christian.[123]

It must be noted that there were a number of boarding schools (pensions)
for girls that developed in Paris between 1850 and 1880, with the number
of lay boarding schools outnumbering the religious. These schools attracted
girls who came from the middle-class, from England as well as the United
States.[124] An examination of French newspapers during that period shows
a number of boarding school advertisements with the curriculum as above
listed indicating the focus of studies for possible candidates. Many of the elite
schools were located on the Right Bank in the northwest part of the Paris, as
was the school that Payne observed.

Payne's insertion of his several visits to the school is not accidental, given
his interest in Wilberforce and as a former school-master in South Carolina
and in Philadelphia. Of special significance for Payne was the fact that the
preceding years in French education were filled with governmental concerns
for universal and secondary education for young women and men. Two important legislative pieces were passed during the time of Payne's European
travels. The first legislation, Le Loi Duruy (Duruy Law), was concerned with
primary education. It ordered that all communities with 500 or more citizens
provide elementary school for it children which implied and included girls.
The second piece of legislation (Circulaire de 30 octobre 1867) incorporated
secondary education for girls. Up to that time secondary education for girls
was restricted to private educational ventures and the church.[125] Payne's insertion of these visits suggests that he was concerned about and advocated the
education of women of color in the United States.[126] While Payne insisted on
an educated black population, this exposure to French Protestant education
only confirmed his thought and practice.

Following the Civil War in the United States, North Americans began
to visit France in great numbers again. Paris was a cultural and intellectual
center. It was the capital of the nineteenth century to some writers reflecting
on the city.[127] During Payne's stay, the Paris Exposition of 1867 was taking
place and literary giants such as Balzac and Diderot were in the newspaper
articles.[128] Taking in the points of interest, Payne's explorations around Paris
included the Louvre, the Pantheon, le Jardin des Plantes, the Bois de Bologne,
the Palais de Luxembourg. Payne was most impressed with the Hotel des In-
valides, the place of Napoleon Bonaparte's ashes. To Payne, the massive red

porphyry sarcophagus in the chapel might be called "the mausoleum of Napoleon."[129] At St. Sulpice Church, Payne commented on viewing the church,

One evening as I was returning to my hotel I stopped to rest at the Church of St. Sulpice, where I noticed several persons adoring the image of the "Immaculate Marie." Upon a marble tablet I read the following inscription and declaration: "Amour, Hommage, , et Reconnaissance a Notre Bonne Mere.

"Mon fils etait atteint de deux malades mortelles. Les secours de l'art n'y pouvaisent rien. Je suis venue prier Marie a cet autel avec confiance, et J'ai obtenu sa guerison. Le 22 Janvier, 1860. A.P.C." ["Love, homage, and gratitude to our good mother. My son was attacked with two mortal diseases. The aid of art could do nothing. I came to beseech Mary at this altar with confidence, and obtained this cure. The 22d of January, 1860. A.P.C."][130]

This huge and imposing edifice dates from 1646. Payne's visit there gave him the opportunity to view three frescoes by the artist Delacroix which had been placed there only six years previous to his Payne's stay in Paris. Although Payne does not comment on it in his autobiography, he would have seen them as he entered the nave of the church as they were and continue to exist in a side chapel upon entering the church.

Throughout this visit to France, Payne continued to be the ambassador for Wilberforce University and the AME Church. He attended the organizational meeting of the Methodist Preacher's Association. It was at this meeting where North American racism appeared to be ever present. Payne stated the following: "...and at my right sat a minister of the M.E. Church, South from Texas, who was soliciting funds for some charitable object in America. This Southern minister must have detested in his heart to sit in such an assemblage by the side of a Negro, but nevertheless he sat there."[131]

But in spite of all these encounters and immersion into French life, Payne's mission to attract benefactors for Wilberforce University was not successful. In his own words: "But, as for my mission, I found that what our Consul had told me, on my first call upon him for advice touching the interests I represented, to be true. The French people were very weary of the applications which agents form America had made for assistance in behalf of the freedmen."[132]

On 18 April 1868, Payne departed from Paris for London and ultimately to Liverpool where he sailed on the "City of Antwerp" for his return to the United States. This period of Payne's European venture comes to an end. While monetary gain was not to be realized in the visit, this voyage and encounter with England, France, and Holland cannot be seen as failure. Payne's diligence in pursuing funds for Wilberforce assisted in giving him entrée to speak with and hear some of the great intellectuals, theologians, educators, and abolitionists of that period. Through lectures, conferences, and touring, Payne was able to complement his own educational interests and curiosity. Further examination of these ventures would allow for comparing and contrasting the experiences within each country: England, financial and theological conversation, spokesperson for the race; Holland, theological conversation and reflection; France, formal continuing education, theological conversation, and educational inquiry. Moreover, Payne was able to experience what it meant to be in places where one was free to be oneself.

In terms of his experiences in Europe, one can see a definitive contrast between his experience as a person of color in the Unites States and a person of color in Europe. At home he was viewed with suspicion, in Europe he was a trusted colleague among his white colleagues; at home his academic and intellectual abilities are questioned, in Europe, he is seen as an intellectual and spokesperson for his denomination; at home, his white colleagues would not venture to acknowledge his presence even within the walls of the church; in Europe, his presence is acknowledged and his words translated as he proclaims the Word of God at the Sunday liturgies in the congregations he visits. At home, he finds it problematic to exist in the midst of his ecclesial tasks; in Europe, he thrives, spiritually and intellectually as the person he is called to be.

Payne's travel in England and France was not a unique one for African Americans traveling in Europe in the nineteenth century. His experience only confirms some of the experiences of those African Americans who were able to Europe before him such as James W.C. Pennington, clergyman and abolitionist, who went to Europe in 1843 to attend the Paris Peace Conference who eventually was awarded a Doctor of Divinity Degree from the University of Heidelberg. James McCune Smith, the first African American physician who received his undergraduate, master's degree from the University of Scotland in Glasgow. He was awarded the M.D. degree in 1837 from the same institution. The dramatist, Victor Séjour, from Louisiana, departed from Louisiana after secondary school and ventured to Paris in 1836 to complete his education and undertake his career in the theatre. William and Ellen Craft escaped to London, England in 1851 and were part of the British abolitionist movement. Frederick Douglass, abolitionist and friend of Payne went to England in 1845 and spoke in Protestant churches about the plight of slave women and men in the United States. Payne's venture to Europe continued a tradition in avenues for African Americans to experience liberation away from North American soil.

RETURN TO THE STATES

Upon his arrival on May 12 in the United States,[133] Payne immediately went to the American Mission Association to talk with Secretary George Whipple.

When Whipple asked him about the success of his trip, Payne had to respond that it had not been successful. There were a number of reasons why the financial appeal had not succeeded. First, Payne did not come immediately after the Civil War when English enthusiasm was high for giving such aid. Second, money had already been sent from England to assist with the new freedmen. Third, some people thought that Wilberforce was a "race" school and some Bishops attending a Pan-Anglican Conference had said they had the means for supporting the school so there was no need for him to come.[134] Charles Smith in *A History of the African Methodist Church 1856–1922* offers another reason for the failure of Payne to raise funds for Wilberforce. Although he respected the esteemed cleric of the church, he felt that Payne with "the strain of aristocracy in his blood" associated and shared the Wilberforce cause with women and men of culture and of the noble classes. Payne didn't go begging with his hands out for support.[135] This could not be Payne's style as President of an institution which was comparable to any of the predominately white institutions in the United States. Wilberforce produced women and men of color with strong academic skills and keen cultural awareness prepared to participate and interact within the North American society as well as the world.

Payne returned to the United States in time to attend the General Conference of 1868. Payne described the meeting as one of excitement because there was discussion about union with the AME Zion Connection. He also presented a report on his travels to Europe. A resolution affirming Payne's presidency of Wilberforce was passed. Thus, he continued to have a dual role within the church, presidency of Wilberforce and the responsibilities of being a Bishop of the church.

It was not until after the Conference that he ventured home to Ohio. On the way he visited Avery College in Pittsburgh as well as some of the common schools in the city. He arrived home on June 11 and wanted to rest. That he did, but soon had enough energy to venture out again to secure faculty for Wilberforce and then head on the road again, observing the schools of the freedmen, and organizing new conferences for the denomination. He was always looking out for the future leadership in the church or more specifically for educated leadership. For example, in 1871, he commented on the meeting of the Pittsburgh conference where there were a number of young energetic men. He observed that three of the men were students of theology at the Presbyterian and Unitarian schools. He was delighted that they were following the regular curriculum for it indicated the future of the rostered ministry in the church.[136] Payne was probably delighted to see that these men were getting a education comparable to what was taking place at Wilberforce. The Theological Department at Wilberforce, in preparing men for ministry, was designed to make pastor-scholars with the use of inductive and deductive methods. There was a spirit of theological inquiry in the classroom where students would be able to discuss and debate in open environment. Payne noted as well, "Our aim is make Christian scholars, not mere book-worms, but workers, educated workers with God for man…"[137]

What was the program for those not pursuing a career in the church? The *Triennial Catalogue of Wilberforce University for the Academic Year 1872–73* notes the Classical, Scientific, and Normal Departments. The Scientific Department included modern languages (French and German) and no classical languages along with the moral and mental philosophy in the latter two years of study. The Classical Department consisted of the traditional strong emphasis on Latin and Greek in the first two years of study. The Normal department emphasized the Oswego method in teacher preparation. The Oswego movement in teacher education stressed student activity and learning by doing.[138] Payne felt that the curriculum that the Wilberforce students experienced was comparable to the courses at any American college.[139] Wilberforce prepared students for professional lives in the American landscape which was its objective from its beginning years as stated in the 1859 catalogue, "…it will be the objective of the teachers to see that the pupil not only knows the lesson, but thoroughly understands it; and by familiar conversations, suggested at the time, so to education the heart and moral feelings, as well as the intellect, as to prepare them for that position designed for them by their Creator."[140]

In addition to the classroom, the life of the student also included regular attendance at chapel to hear scripture, singing, and prayer. Any infraction against good Christian behavior would be met with dismissal. Student behavior was monitored and regular reports sent to the parents.[141] These descriptions of student life were certainly consistent with Payne's commitment to Christian piety and would not meet with his disapproval. In an earlier article he expressed the role of piety by stating "[Piety] is always, at all times, in all places, and in every tongue, spiritual in its meaning; always pointing to the inner man, to the hidden springs of the human soul, indicating his moral complexion, marking his mental attitude towards God and Man….Piety looks through the system of worship, these rites, these ceremonies, the embodiment of the religious idea, into the affections of the individual; nor is she satisfied till the head and heart, the purposes and hopes of the individual are right with God…"[142]

With his work as administrator of Wilberforce and responsibilities in the Episcopal office, Payne continued to correspond with his old professor and theological mentor, President Schmucker of Gettysburg Seminary. Payne, now an educational administrator, conferred with Schmucker, his "venerable preceptor" on occasion. Although a trail of correspondence is not extant, in one piece which has survived, Payne, wrote about previous exchanges as well as advice on an administrative matter, the place and possible audience for the matriculation of students.[143] Although steeped in the AME Church, Payne continued ecclesial kinship with Lutherans.

Although Payne was committed to the Episcopal office and to the presidency of Wilberforce, apparently, there must have been those who were concerned about the direction of the church in his district and wanted him to put more efforts into the district. But an effort to enable Payne to continue with dual responsibilities, the General Conference of 1872 in Nashville, Tennessee, resolved that Payne should not be removed from the presidency of Wilberforce and that he should remain in his district for the following four years.[144] Wilberforce needed a strong scholar and educator in order to hone the church's commitment to education. Payne continued in both roles. His episcopal duties continued with the normal visits to churches within the district as well as speaking to general audiences. During that time he stated that his interest was directed toward the subject of domestic education.

His responsibilities as University president continued to demand attention. He received the $125 balance of a commitment from Chief Justice Chase which was made in 1866. In addition, Wilberforce was a beneficiary of the Avery estate of $10,000 which was given for the education of Black students.[145] His travels in Europe gave Payne increased visibility as well as new friends. In 1873 the Rev. Emile F. Cook,[146] president of the French Methodist Conference, came to visit Payne. While in Paris, Payne visited with him a number of times, and it was his turn to return the hospitality. Cook visited the campus and spoke with students. Dr. Marsh whom Payne had also met in Europe, at the meeting of the Evangelical Alliance, came to visit Payne as well. The friendships and openness of his foreign hosts which Payne experienced in Europe were indeed genuine.

However enthusiastic and dedicated to Wilberforce, Payne, at the General Conference of 1876 in Atlanta, Georgia, he announced his resignation as president as Wilberforce. After thirteen years with dual responsibilities, he intended to complete the work on the history of the AME Church as historiographer of the church and publish some educational works. Payne's responsibility as bishop was changed to the First District. At the meeting of the board of Trustees in June the members accepted the resignation of Payne that was to be effective on the first Wednesday 6 September 1876.[147]

This 1856–76 period concludes where most of the twenty years were lived, at Wilberforce University. These years exhibit a transformation for Payne: from Bishop to university President, from encounters with friends to encounters with political figures, from domestic travel on behalf of the church and university to international ventures in Europe. He continued to be an advocate for education for people of color and immersed himself with his own continuing studies. With all that has transpired, one wonders what can life be for Payne after Wilberforce?

NOTES

1. Payne, *Recollections*, 135; for an extensive examination of the proceedings of the Conference see also, Payne, *History of the A.M.E. Church*, 361–392.
2. Payne, *Recollections*, 140.
3. Ibid., 137.
4. Ibid.
5. Howard Eshbaugh and James Arthur Walther, "Western Seminary" in *Ever a Frontier* (Grand Rapids: Eeermans, 1994), 133–158; William Simmons, "Benjamin Tanner" in *Men of Mark* (Geo. .M. Rewell, 1887, reprint, Johnson Publishing Co., 1970), 985.
6. Payne, *Recollections*, 142.
7. Ibid., 142.
8. See William J. Simmons. *Men of Mark*, 453–456.
9. Payne, *Recollections*, 143.
10. Payne, *Recollections*, 144.
11. Ibid., 145.
12. *Columbia Encyclopedia* assessed 2/27/2009.
13. Carl Schurz. "Biographical Sketch of Carl Schurz" in *Abraham Lincoln* (Cleveland: The Chautauqua Press), 1871.
14. Payne, *Recollections*, 146.
15. Daniel A. Payne, *Welcome to the Ransomed; or, Duties of the Colored Inhabitants of the District of Columbia* (Baltimore: Bull & Tuttle, Clipper Office, 1862).
16. Ibid., 7.
17. Payne, *Recollections*, 14 7.
18. Ibid., 149.
19. "The Accident Aboard the USS Princeton" *Pennsylvania History* (July 1927): 178; see also, *The Liberator* 8 March 1844, *Daily National Intelligencer* 1 March 1844.
20. Franklin, 230; http://www.archives.gov/historical-docs/document.html?doc=7&title.raw=The%20District%20of%20Columbia%20Emancipation%20Act.
21. Payne, *History of the AME Church*, 394.
22. Ibid., 395.
23. Ibid., 142.
24. Payne, *History of the AME Church*, 398.
25. Ibid.
26. Ibid. 399; Payne, *Recollections*, 225.
27. Payne, *Recollections*, 224.

28. Payne, "The History of the Origin and Development of Wilberforce University" in David Smith, *History of the AME Church*. See, also, Payne, *History of the AME Church*, 423—438.

29. Ibid., 100.

30. Ibid., 101.

31. Ibid., 102.

32. Ibid., 103.

33. Ibid., 104.

34. Ibid., 109.

35. The act of April 9, 1852 entitled "an act to enable the trus- s. & c. 2iw, tees of colleges, academies, universities, and other institutions for the purpose of promoting education, to become bodies corporate" in *The Revised States of the State of Ohio*, M.A. Daugherty, John Brasee, George B. Okey, eds. Third Edition, 1883 (Cincinnati: Derby & Co., 1883), 1559 accessed 040909. Google.

36. Ibid., 106.

37. Payne, "Wilberforce," 110.

38. Christopher Hancock, "The Shrimp who Stopped Slavery" *Christian History* 16 Issue 1 (1997):12–19.

39. Payne, "Wilberforce," 111.

40. Joseph C. Hartzell, "Methodism and the Negro in the United States" *Journal of Negro History* 8 No. 3 (July 1923): 308.

41. *Catalogue of the Wilberforce University 1859–60*, (Cincinnati: Methodist Book Concern, 1860).

42. Payne, *Recollections*, 226; Frederick A. McGinnis. *A History and Interpretation of Wilberforce University*. Wilberforce, OH, 1941, 34.

43. Payne, *Recollections*, 153.

44. Ibid., 152.

45. Ibid., 152.

46. Ibid., 153.

47. Ibid.

48. *The Christian Recorder,* 28 March 1863.

49. *The Christian Recorder*, 9 May 1863.

50. *The Christian Recorder*, 28 March 1863.

51. Ibid.; see also *The Christian Recorder*, 15 August 1863.

52. Payne, *Recollections*, 154.

53. Ibid., 155.

54. Ibid., 159.

55. Ibid.

56. Smith, *History of the African Methodist Episcopal Church, vol. II*, 60.

57. Ibid. 154.

58. *The Christian Recorder* 3 March 1866, 5 May 1866.

59. *The Christian Recorder* 15 July 1865.

60. Ibid., 161.

61. Ibid., 162.

62. *The Christian Recorder*, 3 June 1865.

63. Franklin, 246.

64. Eric Foner, *A Short History of Reconstruction* (New York: Harper and Row, 1990), xv.

65. *Recollections*, 167.

66. *Reollections*, 168; Dumas Malone, ed. *Dictionary of American Biography*, s.v. "Phillips, Wendell."

67. Daniel A. Payne, *Semi-Centenary and the Retrospection of the African Meth. Episcopal Church in the United States of America* (Baltimore: Sherwood & Co., 1866; reprint. Freeport, NY: Books for Libraries Press, 1972).

68. Ibid., np.

69. Ibid., "Dedication," np.

70. Ibid., 185.

71. Payne, *Recollections*, 169.

72. Minutes of the Board of Trustees, 16 January 1867.

73. Minutes of the Board of Trustees, 7 March 1867.

74. Payne, *Recollections*, 170.

75. Ancestry.com—U.S. Applications, 1795–1925—Daniel A. Payne, http://search.ancestry.com/cqi-bin/sse.dll?h=1553340&db=USpassports&indiv=1.

76. Ibid., 171.

77. Ibid., 173.

78. Ibid., 174.

79. William Fullerton. *Charles Haddon Spurgeon: A Biography* (Chicago: Moody Bible Institute, 1966, rev. from 1920).

80. Arthur Penryhn Stanley, *Historical Memorials of Westminster Abbey* (Philadelphia: George W. Jacobs & Co., 1899); Rowland E. Prothero, *The Life and Correspondence of Arthur Penrhyn* (New York: Charles Schribner's Sons, 1893); Anthony A. Aglen, ed. *A Selection from the Writings of Dean Stanley* (New York: Charles Scribner's Sons, 1894).

81. Ibid., 179.

82. *New York Times*, 22 September 1867.

83. See Adrain R. Bailey, David C. Harvey, and Catherine Brace, "Disciplining Youthful Methodist Bodies in Nineteenth-Century Cornwall" *Annals of the Association of American Geographers* 97 (March 2007): 142–157; Brian Harrison, *Drink and the Victorians* (Pittsburgh: University of Pittsburg Press, 1971).

84. Ibid., 179.

85. Ibid., 175.

86. Ibid., 193.

87. Ibid., 194.

88. Ibid., 177.

89. Ibid., 176.

90. *L'Evangeliste,* 8 août 1867, 15 août 1867, 22 août 1867.

91. Payne, *Recollections*, 183.

92. *L'Evangeliste*, 8 août 1867. Translation by author.

93. The 15 août 1867 edition of the *L'Evangeliste* had the following new clip: "One heard equally in this session, and with great interest, a bishop of color, the

Rev. Dr. Payne a member of the African Methodist Church in the United States. We reproduced, in our last edition, a part of the discussion which he delivered before the Committee on Missions Abroad." Translation by author.

94. 15 août 1867, *Evangeliste.*

95. *Recollections*, 188–189; see also *L'Evangeliste*,6 Septembre 1867.

96. Ibid., 191; see also, 19 et 26 Septembre *L'Evangeliste*, 282.

97. Rev. Edward Steade, *Proceedings of The Amsterdam Conference of the Evangelical Alliance, Held in August, 1867* (London: Office of the Evangelical Alliance, 1868), xvi.

98. Ibid., vii-viii.

99. *Le Protestant Libéral* 5 septembre 1867.

100. Ibid; see also, H.B. Smith, "America: Report on the State of Religion in the United States" in *Proceedings*, 217–243.

101. *Le Protestante Libéral*, 5 septembre 1867; Payne, *Recollections*, 191.

102. Ibid.,192.

103. *L'Evangeliste* 29 août 1867, *L'Espérance* 6 septembre.

104. Ibid.; *L'Espérance*, 6 septembre 1867.

105. *Special Report of the Antislavery Conference* (London: British and Foreign Antislavery Societies, 1887), 26.

106. Samuel Macauley Jackson, ed. *The New Schaff-Herzog Encyclopedia of Religious Knowledge* (New York: Funk and Wagnalls), s.v. "Cook, Emile Francis;" Conférence Méthodiste Française. Consécration de M. Emile-F Cook in *Varia 1854–56* (Paris: L'Agence des Publications Méthodistes, 1854).

107. Payne, *Recollections*, 195.

108. "Annual Meeting of the Board of Trustees," 10 October 1867, 28 January 1868.

109. Ibid., 17 December 1867.

110. Payne, *Recollections*, 196.

111. Ibid., 196, 204.

112. The Sorbonne was established in 1253 beginning the faculty of Theology and named after Robert de Sorbon, confessor to the King Saint Louis; see also, http://www.sorbonne.fr/document173.html?173; Y. Gaulupeau, *La France à l'école* (Découverte Gallimard), 1992.

113. The College de France was established by François I in 1530 to teach subject areas not offered at the the Sorbonne; see also, http://www.college-de-france.fr/default/EN/all/college_english/index.htm.

114. Ibid., 204; see also Manus Magnusson, ed. *Cambridge Biographical Dictionary*, s.v. "Pressense" Raoul Stephan, *Histoire du Protestantisme Francais* (Paris: Librairie Artheme, 1961), 236, 267,283, 271; *Le Protestant Libéral*, le 14 août 1867, le 31 octobre 1867.

115. Laboulaye was a lawyer and at one time was head of the French anti-slavery Society. He was also the administrator of the College de France; see Mercer Cook, "Edouard de Laboulaye and the Negro" *The Journal of Negro History* 18 (July 1933): 246–255; Serge Gavronsky, "American Slavery and the French Liberals an Interpretation of the Role of Slavery in French Politics During the Second Empire" *Journal of Negro History* 51 (January 1966): 36–52.

116. *Recollections.* 197.

117. Ibid.;*Cambridge Biographical Dictionary*, s.v. Quatrefages; see also his research which includes *Les Polynésiens et Leur Migrations* (Paris: Libraire de la Société de Géographie, 1864) and *Rapport sur les Progrès de L'Anthropologie* (Paris: L'Imprimerie Impérial, 1867).

118. *Recollections*, 197; see also, *Histoire du Protestantisme Français*, 283–4, 327; Jean-François Zorn «Il y a cent ans Eugène Casali » *Mission* 11 (Mars 1991): 9; Eugene Casalis, *Mes Souvenirs* (Paris: Fischbacher, 1884).

119. Payne, *Recollections*, 197; In this statement Payne exhibits the nuances of the French language which characterized Solomon as "a tall man" as well as "a great man." See also, David Nicholls, "The Wisdom of Salomon: Myth or Reality?" *Journal of Interamerican Studies and World Affairs* 20 (November 1976): 377–392.

120. Payne, *Recollections*, 199.

121. A. Decoppet, *Paris Protestant* (Paris: J. Bonhoure et Cie, 1876).

122. Eugène Bersier, *Recueil de Souvenirs de la Vie d'Eugene Bersier* (Paris: Librairie Fischbacher,nd), 222.; see also Eugene Bersier, *Histoire du Synode Generale de L'Eglise Reformee de France* (Paris: Sandoz et Fischbacher, 1872), iii; A. Boegner, Varia #13919; *L'Église Evangélique de Neuilly-sur-Seine et son Premier Pasteur 1864 à 1889;* Eugène Bersier. Revue du Mois in *Revue Chrétienne* XIV (Août 1867): 504–512.

123. *L'Espérance*, le 8 novembre 1867.

124. Rebecca Rogers, *From the Salon to the Classroom.* University Park, PA: Penn State University Press, 2005, 168.

125. Yves Gaulupeau, *La France à L'Ecole*, (Paris: Découvertes Gallimard, 1992), 76; Françoise Lelièvre and Claude Lelièvre, *Histoire de la scolarisation des filles* (Paris: Nathan, 1991), 76–84; *Ecole,* le 15 juillet 1867, le 1 octobre 1867, le 15 novembre; *Le Protestant Libéral*, le 31 octobre 1867; Claude Lelièvre, *Histoire des Institutions Scolaires (1789–1989)* (Paris: Nathan 1990).

126. David Wills, "Woman and Domesticity in the A.M.E. Tradition: The Influence of Daniel Alexander Payne," in *Black Apostles at Home and Abroad*, David W. Wills and Richard Newman, eds. (Boston: G.K. Hall and Co., 1982): 133–146.

127. See, Patrice Higgonet, *Paris: Capital of the World* (Cambridge: President and Fellows of Harvard College, 2002); Walter Benjamin "Paris, the Capital of the Nineteenth Century" in *Reflections* (New York: Schocken Press), 1978.

128. Henry Bluemthal, *American and French Culture, 1800–1900*, (Baton Rouge: Louisiana State University, 1975), 31; *Le Figaro*, 29 janvier 1868, 6 juin 1867, 17 mai 1867.

129. Ibid., 200.

130. Payne, *Recollections*, 197.

131. Ibid., 201.

132. Ibid.

133. http://search.ancestry.com/cqi-bin/sse.dll?h=6251173&db=nypl&indiv=1.

134. Ibid., 202.

135. Smith, 76.

136. Ibid., 205.

137. Ibid., 121.

138. *Triennial Catalogue of Wilberforce University for the Academic Year 1872–73* (Xenia, OH: Torchlight Steam Printing House, 1873), 18–19; see also, Joel Spring, *The American School 1642–1990* (New York: Longman, 1990).

139. Payne, "*Wilberforce*," 120.

140. *Catalogue of the Wilberforce University 1859–60*, (Cincinnati: Methodist Book Concern, 1860), 11.

141. Ibid., 17.

142. Daniel A. Payne, "Religion and Piety" in *Repository of Religion and Literature* (July 1858): 72–75.

143. Daniel A. Payne to Samuel S. Schmucker 30 March 1969.

144. Payne, *Recollections*, 211.

145. Minutes of the Trustees of Wilberforce University, 5 April 1867.

146. Conférence Méthodiste Française, *Consécration de M. Emile-F Cook* in *Varia 1854–56* (Paris: L'Agence des Publications Méthodistes, 1854), 3,8.

147. Minutes of the Trustees of Wilberforce University 14 June 1876; *Recollections*, 218.

Chapter Four

The Waning Years: 1877–1893

In some ways, Payne's life changed radically since he did not have the dual responsibilities of bishop and university administrator. But, in many ways, his life remained the same with the on-going themes of his professional adult life. Payne continued to be an ecclesiastical leader in the AME Church as one of its bishops engaged with all the storms and stresses of that office. He continued to be the advocate of education and demonstrated his love of learning with his own self-education. He continued to travel at home and abroad; he continued to be a person engaged in life within the church.

CHANGING RESPONSIBILITIES AND INFLUENCE

Payne continued to be respected as an educator. During the 1876–1877 academic year, there was a presidential search for Howard University. An editorial essay in the 22 February 1877 issue of *The Christian Recorder*, advocated that Payne should be considered for the presidency of Howard University in the nation's capitol. It listed several reasons for this recommendation: his solid reputation among blacks and whites, his strong and high moral character, his experience as a college administrator, his contributions as a scholar, and his large following through his travels and networking in the church which would attract students. Moreover, it would be good to have a black man as president of a black institution.[1] There is no documentary evidence of his response. Perhaps he felt his energies were directed more toward denominational matters or that his commitment was directed toward Wilberforce which he helped to develop and administer prior to his retirement. Besides that a number of issues needed a Bishop's input in the AME Church and Payne was in the midst of them.

In May of the same year, the General Conference was held in Atlanta, Georgia. At this meeting, there were "numerous petitions from interested parties" requesting the continuation of Payne as president of Wilberforce University. The history doesn't show that any official action was taken about this matter. At the same meeting, in anticipation of the announcement of an Ecumenical Methodist Conference, in London England, in September 1881, Payne was one of eleven delegates designated to attend.[2] In addition, the Conference highlighted with enthusiasm, the work of the MITE group, which was the women's association dealing with missions of the church.

Later in the same year, Payne continued his ever-present appeal for education in the church. In an announcement about the coming Philadelphia Conference, Payne made an announcement indicating that he anticipated meeting with the constituency to consider the interests of education in the District as well as to establish a Literary and Historical Association.[3] More specific work at the Conference is outlined a week later when the pastors were instructed to come prepared to respond to the following: the number of members in their congregations, the number of those members who can read the Bible, the number of subscribers to the *Christian Recorder*, the best ways to promote Christian Education at Wilberforce University, the promotion of Christian education in the Book Concern, and the manner of disseminating biblical knowledge within the membership of the AME Church.[4] One sees from these announcements that Payne's concern for education spanned the various arenas of the ministry, from the congregation to the university levels. How might the churches promote biblical literacy among the adults? These issues also indicated the important role of the pastor in promoting education in the local congregational settings and the importance of and respect for an educated laity. The local congregation was the locus for religious conversation and reflection. The parish pastor would need to be the educational leader and advocate.

The abilities and gifts of Payne were also noted in an editorial sent to President Haynes imploring him to consider the appointment of Payne along with two other persons of color to be part of the Commission of fifty persons representing the United States at the Paris Industrial Exhibition in 1878. The editorial went on to say that inasmuch as persons of color have been on the land even before many whites, have aided in the struggle for the republic in 1776 and most recently in the Civil War, there is no doubt that they should be represented as part of the delegation. Besides, they emphasized that in France, there was no regard to color. In addition, these men are scholarly, with experience, and are fluent in the French language.

In addition, since they were now citizens, couldn't they not enjoy some of the spoils of that that status?[5]

An examination of his journal entries for the two years following his resignation (1877 and 1878) indicates his movement and thinking on these matters. For example, in 14 August 1877, he shared his schedule for the day. He preached in an AME congregation in Princeton, New Jersey in the morning and in the afternoon, he spoke to the Sunday school children. In the evening he heard a Pastor Buff and gave some words to the people. On the previous day, he was in Brooklyn and visited with several people and pastors, arriving in Princeton, at 9 o'clock that evening.[6]

As was the case in his earlier years he visited educational institutions. On 16 August 1877 while in Princeton, New Jersey, he toured the Princeton campus and commented on its president, Dr. McCosh whom he considered one of the great scholars of the time as well as Dr. Hodge whom he considered the greatest theologian that the U.S. had produced.[7]

Payne always expected the best from his students at Wilberforce; in the same way he expected excellence from the clergy under his leadership. Visiting churches under his care, he was ever critical of the preaching that he heard for its proclamation Word. In his journal entry of 18 August 1877, he wrote about a visit to one of the AME churches in Huntington, Long Island,

> Sunday morning the 19th I visited our little flock, and heard brothers Javis and Taylor, two exhorters. They tried to preach but utterly failed. The former is the more intelligent. His theme was "Jonah the Prophet." The latter was exceedingly incoherent; made use of meaningless expressions. This is disgraceful to the Christian ministry that such men should occupy its pulpit. There were about 3 or 4 persons in attendance, one man and one woman turned their backs against the speakers.[8]

We can also examine his personal routines after Wilberforce as well. We see a person who is engaged with this work and responsibilities, and at the same time with his own self-education. For example, on 23 August 1877 he wrote a letter to President B.J. Lee, postcard to a Liervoi, and a Shuffler. On the previous evening he wrote that the preacher in one of the AME churches on the Nature and Position of Man in the Universe based on Genesis Chapter 1: 26–28. He visited people in the village. He left Jamaica and arrived in Brooklyn, Long Island. He wrote letters, visited with individuals and in the evening he attended one of the AME churches on Bridge Streets where friends devoted many hours to the Sunday School.

In an August 1877 entry he communicated his on-going self-education. On 30 August 1877 he wrote:

Jeudi J'étudiais la Sainte Bible aussi la Botanie et la littérature française, c'est dire les études historiques par M. Le Vicomte Châteaubriand.
[Thursday. I studied the Holy Bible; also Botany and French Literature, that is to say, Historic Studies by the Vicomte Chateaubriand.][9]

On 26 September 1877 he wrote,

J'étudiais la Sainte Bible dans la langue française; aussi la botanie et l'analysis de la grammaire anglaise.
[I studied the Holy Bible in French; also botany and Analysis of English Grammar.][10]

His engagement with education was not only communal but individual. This isn't strange for in the days of his youth, he had developed self-study habits. Throughout his journals he wrote the entries in French and in English intentionally continuing to utilize his language skills which he had acquired in France during his European travels. It appeared that he continued to have affection for the language and the country. An examination of his personal Journal of 1878 shows that it was written in a similar vain, in French and in English, identifying his travels and visits with pastors and congregations as well as his personal professional readings.

Payne's commitment to congregational life in the AME Church was confirmed in an announcement to the clergy of the church in which he urges, or perhaps a better word might be, commanded the pastors of the church to purchase the new hymn book of the AME church. He announced the following to pastors in his district:

This is to inform you, that the New Hymn book has just been issued from the Press and Book Binder. It is an excellent compilation of hymns and spiritual songs, fully up to the times, with lyrics for all the subject, that come within the range of Christian worship. You are therefore, *instructed* to lay aside, not only every other hymn-book, which you have been using in the pulpit, belonging to other denominations, but, also, to lay aside our old hymn book which is now obsolete and send in your orders for the new. Let your orders be large enough to supply every member of your charges with a copy. *Do this immediately*—because we all need to its spiritual treasures, while the Publisher needs the money to pay for them. *We hope you will be prompt in heeding these instructions.*[11]

Inasmuch as we see Payne ever engaged in the life of the church, the times were changing. The strong influence which characterized his years of leadership up to this point began to wane. Coan in his examination of those years writes, "From 1840, the year that Payne became a member of the African Methodist Episcopal Church, to 1876, he exerted dominating influence in determining the denominational policies. And from 1876 to his death in 1893, his influenced slowly declined."[12]

Coan identifies three factors that were central to this lessening of power and influence. The first factor was the changing venue of education in the formation and development of clergy in the church. There were a number of institutions which were developed following the Civil War in which persons could receive primary as well as theological education. There were an increased number of clergy who were educated generally and theologically. A second factor was the changing emphasis of the AME Church as it now focused more on the expansion of its missionary efforts. There was a desire to expand denominational ministry in various parts of the world. The third factor that Coan identifies is that of "the low tone of morality, characteristic of post-war politics" which even spread to the clergy of the denomination.[13]

Some of the historically black educational institutions that started after the Civil War include: Shaw University in Raleigh in 1865; Morehouse College in Atlanta in 1867 and Benedict in Columbia, South Carolina in 1871, all started by the Baptist Church; Morgan State in Baltimore in 1867 and Clark Atlanta in 1870, started by the Methodist Episcopal Church; St. Augustine's in Raleigh, NC in 1867 begun by the Episcopal Church. The formation of these schools indicated the missionary zeal of the denominations for the education of the newly freed women and men. In addition, the denominations expanded the scope of their educational interests from providing only elementary education to providing opportunities for higher education. Howard University was charted by the government of the United States in 1867.[14] "For the sake of these churches that were to be, they took measures to build up schools of higher learning at carefully chosen centers, which they hoped might become favorite resorts for scholars, rallying points for religious organization and institutions of Christian culture and enlightenment for all the region around."[15]

It was hoped that these institutions would give Black students an education that was comparable to his or her white counterpart. The curriculum included: Latin, Greek, mathematics, science, philosophy, history, astronomy, English composition, and literature. "Black leaders concurred that tomorrow's African American clergymen, lawyers, physicians, statesmen, and businessmen, not less than their white peers, needed to acquire learning in the academic traditions of the past; and they stoutly resisted suggestions that rudimentary industrial and agricultural training was a more realistic alternative."[16]

Although Payne was an advocate and pioneer in education, he was cautious in terms of the expansion of educational institutions sponsored by the AME Church. For him, it was a matter of financial prudence. By 1881, the AME Church supported six colleges. He thought these institutions were less than credible as institutions of higher learning. Coan viewed this attitude by

Payne as restricted for he wanted the denomination to focus on Wilberforce so that it could be a first-class institution. Coan wrote, "He wanted the entire denomination to concentrate upon this project."[17] One wonders if the correct editing would better read, "He wanted the entire denomination to concentrate on his (Payne's) project."

There was clearly a concern by the leadership for the expansion of the denomination, not only within the United States but abroad as well. Coan notes that "[t]he dominating interest of the African Methodist Episcopal Church during the last four decades of the nineteenth century was expansion."[18] A comparative analysis of the growth of the denomination can be seen in the parochial reports of the General Conferences of 1864 with eight Annual Conferences and 1880 with thirty annual conferences. In 1864 the membership was 50,000; traveling preachers, 500; local preachers, 2000; churches, 1600; colleges, one; schools, many. The statistics in 1880 indicated: membership, 306,044 communicants, 81,522 non-communicants; traveling preachers, 1717; local preachers, 3907; churches, 2051; school, 88 school houses; parsonages, 395; Sunday schools, 9346; Sunday School Teachers, 14,990; Sunday School Scholars, 154,549.

The 1880s brought expansion not only domestically to the denomination but also internationally. While the mission work in Haiti was going well, there was a desire to expand the work of the church over the African continent.[19] Although previous work in Liberia (started by Bishop J.P. Campbell in 1824) and Sierra Leone (started by Bishop Daniel Coker in the first half of the 19th century),[20] had been abandoned, there was a desire to begin again in Liberia. Again, Payne voiced restraint in such expansion. Already invested in Haiti, the church should concentrate on making that mission site strong and healthy. As Coan writes, "…the needs are many. Payne held that they were in need of a physician, a mechanic, and agriculturist and a specialist in languages."[21] However passionate Payne might have been in his request, Bishop Turner traveled to Sierra Leone and eventually organized the first Annual Conference on the African continent which took place in 1891.

In May of 1881, the General Conference was held in Atlanta, Georgia. At this meeting, there were "numerous petitions from interested parties" requesting the continuation of Payne as president of Wilberforce University. The history doesn't show that any action was taken about this matter.

Although his influence was waning, Payne continued to confront issues. An examination of the General Conference of 1880 illustrates his energy. One of the delegates to the General Conference from New Jersey was not able to attend due to illness, so Payne selected the Rev. J.G. Yeiser to be the replacement. When Yeiser arrived in St. Louis, Missouri, the Conference refused to seat him. Payne filed a protest to the General Conference. In summary, Payne's argument:

1. The law regulating the composition of the General Conference does not recognize any alternates to ministerial delegates; therefore it does not order any method to create them.
2. The election of alternates to ministerial delegates is mere custom, but custom without law is not binding. It is often nothing more than antiquated error.
3. The appointment of Rev. J. G. Yeiser was the product of an emergency not foreseen by law; therefore it is not forbidden by the law and consequently cannot be a canonical office.
4. To punish an officer for an act not forbidden by law is unjust and cruel. For such reasons I enter my most solemn protest, and beg that it be put on the record of the General Conference.[22]

Yeiser was seated.

Another issue which illustrated the changing tide of leadership within the AME Church during Payne's post-Wilberforce years was the issue of organic union with the British Methodist Episcopal Church in Canada which had separated from the AME Church in America in 1856. At the General Conference meeting in 1880 there was interest on the part of the Canadian church in uniting again with the African Methodist Episcopal Church through mission endeavors. Smith reported, "A commission was created to meet the General Conference of the British Methodist Episcopal Church for the purpose of arranging and effecting a *modus operandi* of cooperation in the missionary work in the West Indies and British Guiana, such cooperation to be known as the 'Reunion of the African Methodist Episcopal and British Methodist Episcopal Churches in the America.'"[23] The conference, in addition, approved the following resolution submitted by Bishop Turner:

> *Resolved,* That in the event of an agreement of terms of union between the Commission of the African Methodist Episcopal Church and the General Conference of the British Methodist Episcopal Church being satisfactorily adjusted, the terms of union shall be submitted to the several Annual Conferences, and the adoption of the terms by two thirds of said Annual Conferences shall be regarded as binding.[24]

At the General Conference of 1884, Payne protested against the organic union of the AME Church with the British Methodist Episcopal Church. The following year, he had to appear before the court to testify about the organization of the British Methodist Episcopal Church as the court decided on the ownership of properties of the respective churches. Payne was against this organic union because it would place an additional financial burden on the AME Church because the British Methodist Episcopal Church would be admitted by absorption and that would not be unification. There would not be the unification by two equals.[25] Coan pointed out that Payne was concerned about the added cost of $9300 each year. There were too many financial obligations on United States soil to take on this additional cost.[26]

A SECOND VOYAGE TO EUROPE

The time for Payne's departure for Europe arrived. With his passport issued on 30 June 1881, on 9 July 1881, Payne sailed on the "Egypt" and made his second voyage to Europe as delegate to the Methodist Ecumenical Conference in London, England.[27] The ship arrived in Liverpool on 19 July. As in his previous trip, Payne encountered old acquaintances, worshipped in congregations, and toured in England and in Paris, France.

The first two days on land, Payne remained in Liverpool where he went as a visitor to the Wesleyan Methodist Conference which began on July 18. From there he traveled to London and met old friends. Payne mentioned his time with Dr. Frederick J. Jobson who was an architect, minister, and painter. Payne had five of Jobson's works in his own library. Jobson was president of the Conference and also Book Steward (responsible for the printing of denominational printing and sale of books). Payne stated that Jobson was "a man of varied accomplishments—for he was an architect and a painter in oil and water colors...As a pulpit orator his qualities were of the noblest kind."[28] Payne departed from London and ventured to the cathedral in Canterbury which he found rich in the medieval past.

Payne was not able to spend an extensive time in France, but did explore some of the places he remembered visiting during his first voyage and found time to visit friends and scholars. Two of those friends had died since that previous trip: Dr. Jean-Louis Vallette, educator, pastor of l'Eglise des Billettes and head of the Lutheran Church died in 1872[29] and the Rev. Emile Cook who visited Payne at Wilberforce and addressed the students died in 1874. Payne's former landlord's M. and Mme. Moindron were still there as well as Professor Quatrefages. Quaterfages gave Payne a copy of his latest research work *L'Espece Humaine*. Payne had already worked through *Rapport sur les Progres de l'Anthropologie* and at the time of writing his autobiography, Payne was reading *Les Polynesiens et leurs Migrations*.[30] Apart from these personal visits, he revisited cultural sites including the Zoological Gardens.

After his short stay in Paris, Payne returned to England where he returned to Canterbury and then ventured to the Springs of Harrowgate, Sunderland where he preached in the Presbyterian Church. He also went to Glasgow, Edinburgh, and York where he saw the cathedral, before returning to London.

The delegates to the conference were treated to breakfast at Exeter Hall on the morning of September 6 which was followed by introductions and short speeches, including one by Payne. After singing, prayers and the benediction, Payne departed with the other members of the United States delegation and visited Windsor Castle.

The genesis for this Methodist Ecumenical Conference emerged from the Methodist Episcopal General Conference that had met in Baltimore in 1876 which called for a meeting of all expressions of Methodism. From the opening session on the next day 7 September, Payne was immersed in the work of the church, within the conference sessions as well as in the life of the churches in the surrounding areas. At the noon session on 12 September Payne presented a paper entitled, "Relations of Methodism to the Temperance Movement." In this essay Payne reminded the delegates of the Methodist strong defense against intemperance. Temperance for Methodists was not an afterthought but a fundamental first principle.[31] He reminded them as well of the root of the word which came from the Greek meaning "self-control" which one should practice especially in those things that are destructive to the body.

In addition to preparing and presenting his paper, Payne also presided over one of the morning sessions of 17 September 1881. In the session, "Foreign Missions" was the theme for the participants. Payne could only say, in regard to his competence and responsibility of presiding at the session, "How I discharged this honor let others say."[32]

Payne divided his time between the conference and the community outside of the deliberations. He preached one Sunday morning at Lady Marguerite Road Chapel. He presented the educational work among the free women and men at the Tunbridge Wells Wesleyan Church and shared the present conditions of the former slaves emphasizing the political, industrial, and social perspectives during the period of reconstruction.[33] Furthermore, he made social contact through dinner invitations and teas that took place. Naturally, he took in some of the cultural sites like art galleries and museums. In the midst of the thought-provoking theological discussions and interesting social encounters, news arrived that President Garfield of the United States had been assassinated. With that news, a pall was drawn over all the representatives. With the conclusion of the conference on 20 September, Payne boarded the steamship "Erin" and departed from Liverpool on 21 September for New York.

The return voyage might have been pleasant except for two incidents. First, although they ship departed in clear weather after a couple of days the sea became rough causing a number of people to become sea-sick. This lasted for about a week. Payne must have recalled the aborted voyage he experienced in 1846. The second incident involved worship. Payne asked the captain whether there was going to be Sunday worship. The captain informed him that he as captain was responsible for that, which he did by reading from the

Anglican Book of Prayer. At the end of the service, the captain left. This was repeated on the following Sunday with the addition of some Sankey hymns.[34] Payne remarked that he didn't offer anyone the opportunity to preach and there were four clergymen on board; however, they were men of color.[35] So again, racism marred a voyage. Payne disembarked from the ship on 4 October 1881 with its arrival into the New York harbor.[36]

The following year 1882 was a one of celebration in Payne's life. It was the thirtieth anniversary of his election to the office of bishop in the AME Church. The three day celebration, 11–13 May, took place at the Sullivan Street African Methodist Church in New York.[37] A banquet honoring Payne was hosted by the congregation. Short speeches were offered by a number of bishops as well as some laity. A remarkable observation was noted in the history of the denomination. When Payne was elected bishop, not one person who had a degree, whether undergraduate or honorary. There in the midst of the banquet sat 17 clergy with degrees coming from 17 states. While it was a celebrative event, it proved to be a literary event as well, with essays delivered to the group. Certainly this type of event was indicative of the influence of Payne's lifelong passions and practices in the life of the denomination.

In terms of scholarly accomplishment, the publication of Payne's work *Domestic Education* was announced to the members of the General Conference in 1885. This was Payne's contribution to the field of religious education. Coan states that "[t]he book is an exposition on the need, the aim, the methods and the results of Christian education in the home." Based on the wisdom of Proverbs 22:6 "Train up a child in the way he should go, and when he is old he will not depart from it," Payne locates the base of Christian education within the family. For him, "Christian education is divinely designed not to confer exclusive privileges upon any chosen people; but to enlighten, improve, and develop into perfection humanity as a whole unbroken unit, consequently to develop into the highest possible human perfection every child of Adam."[38] This description of education certainly confirms Payne's identification with the Methodist theological tradition, specifically with the doctrine of sanctification and the Christian's striving toward perfection in this life. This education takes place through the family. For him, the family may be natural father and mother, but Payne extends that to include: aunt, uncle, grandparents, who might take the place of the parents.[39] The family is the "miniature Church" as well as the "miniature state" for the child. From within the family, Payne sees the following essential components: communication between the father and mother in order to present an univocal word to the child, family worship, private prayer, and the self-culture of the parents in which they model the Christian life. The important motif here is an environment in which the child is allowed to flourish. When these components are in sync, Payne believes the child can be successfully trained in his or her Christian formation.[40] The outside sources most cited are those of Alexander Vinet and Frederich Froebel,[41] two continental scholars. Although the work cites these and other scholars, one must say that the work emerges from Payne's own life story: nurturing from his family and relatives, and pastoral care, numerous visitations into the homes of families as pastor and bishop in the United States and abroad.

In addition to his views on Christian education, Payne also inserted hymns that were original in text (his words) and music that underscored the importance of home, family, and the nurture of children. The titles include: "Personal and Home Consecration" in two versions, "The Consecrated Home," "Reveal Thyself to Me," "Hymn for the Consecration of Children," "Consecration of an Infant Son," and "Consecration of an Infant Daughter."[42]

In 1888, the eighteenth General Conference took place in Indianapolis, Indiana. It was a conference that was significant in that Payne preached three sermons during the assembly: the Sacramental, Quadrennial, and Ordination. Smith reports that this was the first time that this had occurred. Now over seventy-seven years of age, he appeared to be strong and as energetic in his homiletic delivery as the younger clerics. The editor indicated that the sermons were not from a manuscript but delivered extemporaneously.[43]

The Quadrennial Sermon delivered on May 10 was based on Malachi 2: 4–7, a text which enabled him to concentrate on the ministry; comparing and contrasting the Jewish priesthood and the Christian ministry. The educational preparation needed for ministry comes through in stating:

> Then there are these two qualities which ought to be possessed by every man, whether he be licentiate, deacon, elder, or bishop:
> He must have the capacity to take in knowledge as a sponge absorbs water, and must make what he takes in a part of himself; must be active, and have the capacity to develop his activity. He must have a good memory, and what he learns must be engraved on his heart; he must love it, live it, and then give it out on his lips to the people. These are the qualities which every man who desires to be a minister should have: He should in all things emulate the great Teacher.[44]

On May 24, Payne delivered the Ordination sermon. This sermon was based on Isaiah 11: 1–10, centering on the genealogy of Jesus, from the stem of Jesse; he urges those to be ordained to model their lives after the ministry of Jesus. Ever mindful of the social unrest which brought the Civil War and the aftermath of racial unrest that continued to plague the nation, he states, that they are to center their lives on the Gospel.

Yes, the gospel shall cover the earth as the waters cover the sea. This is what you are to teach. Do not try to set race against race. This is the work of the devil, not of Christ. You must not see the white man against the black man, nor the brown man against the yellow man; but harmonize them all, and teach them to walk in peace. It is your work to teach the gospel of the Lord Jesus Christ—that he died for all.[45]

He underscores this urgency by declaring, "Study him, study him as your model; study the perfect model of manhood until he shall be conformed in you. Finally, my brethren, I say to you in the words of St. Paul: 'Be strong in the Lord, and in the power of his might.' Amen, and amen.

It was at this Conference that Payne presented the *History of the AME Church*, research for which he had begun in the late 1840s as historiographer of the AME Church. Coan wrote that he resigned as president of Wilberforce in 1876 in order to complete the task. Now in 1888, he submitted the manuscript for publication to the General Conference. Payne submitted it with the following proposal for the Conference's deliberations:

This is to inform you that the history of the African Methodist Episcopal Church is completed. I was authorized by the General Conference of 1848 to write it. In searching for material, in arranging, in sifting the chaff from the wheat, and in putting all that is valuable in historic form, forty years have been consumed. The General Conference of 1856 ordered that when completed the Book Concern should publish it, and that I should be rewarded for my labors by a royalty of 25 per cent. At my advanced age this royalty would be of little or no profit to me, and, therefore, I beg that the order of the General Conference of 1856 be annulled and a new and different arrangement made with the Historiographer.[46]

Payne valued the manuscript to be five thousand dollars. His proposal as sent to a committee which concluded that Payne would receive two thousand dollars for the manuscript along with the right to supervise and control its publication.[47]

With all that he accomplished in 1888 up to and including the General Conference, Payne's productivity continued with the completion of his autobiography, *Recollections of Seventy Years.* This was accomplished with the assistance of his secretary, Sarah Brice, and the editing by Bishop C.S. Smith. This book is an invaluable resource in reconstructing his life story, but one must agree with Coan's assessment that "[t]he great shortcoming lies in the fact that there are many unexplained allusions which leave the reader in doubt."[48] The work consists of his reflections on his life from infancy through his seventy-seventh year. One can only be in awe of his encounters and engagement with a whole host of people, from the illiterate slave to the great statesmen and savants of his day, from his congregational life in Charleston, South Carolina to the great cathedrals of Europe.

The concluding paragraphs of his life story are interesting in that he returned to the beginning years of his life and tells of the importance of education which led him to accomplishments he would have never imagined. From his encounter with Bachmann, the Lutheran pastor, while head of his school in South Carolina to his coming north to study at the Lutheran Seminary in Gettysburg, Payne could only marvel:

> That worm! that worm! that curious, beautiful worm! "The Lord reigneth" in the heavens and in the earth. The former truth is admitted by all thoughtful men; but comparatively few, even of professing Christians, see the Almighty Hand in the small and ordinary affairs of men. From that worm sprung up an acquaintance with that great naturalist who gave me those letters of introduction to the Lutheran clergy, who placed me in the theological seminary at Gettysburg, which prepared me for the enlarged usefulness of more than fifty-three years. As an educator thou didst lead me from Charleston, S. C., to Philadelphia, Pa.; from Philadelphia to Washington, D. C.; from Washington to Baltimore, and from Baltimore to Wilberforce, O. Over Northern lands, over Southern States, over foreign countries, back to my native State, through storm and calm, through dangers seen and unseen—in the sweltering South, back to the freezing North. Where next, O thou Giver of life, thou Author of all its possibilities—where next?[49]

In the context of all the accolades addressed to Payne,[50] with all the accomplishments he achieved with the publication of important works from his research, the latter part of the decade brought the sting of death upon Payne, with the death of his wife Eliza. At the age of seventy-four she died on 24 August 1888. The cause of death as noted on the death certificate was old age. She was buried in Massies Creek Cemetery, Green County, Ohio.

By the end of the decade Payne had traveled to Europe for the second time, completed three major writing projects and became a widower. With all that, there was still more to accomplish.

In 1891, the Ecumenical Methodist Conference was held in Washington, D.C. Payne was a member of the delegation from the African Methodist Episcopal Church.[51] The minutes indicate Payne's active participation in the conference but do not state explicitly the nature of his involvement. The beginning years of the 90s also brought another honor to Payne. The Board of Trustees of Wilberforce, recognizing the continued need for educated clergy within the denomination expanded the Theology department by creating a committee to study the feasibility of theological seminary. At the Board meeting in session in 1891, it approved the development of the seminary in the name of the denomination's senior bishop, Daniel A. Payne. He went on to become the first Dean of the seminary. The formation of the seminary certainly complemented Payne's passions in education in the general sphere with Wilberforce University and in the theological sphere with the establishment of Payne Seminary.[52]

From May 2 through May 24, 1892, the nineteenth General Conference of the church took place in Philadelphia, Pennsylvania. It was at this gathering that on May 13 that the Conference celebrated Payne's forty years as a Bishop with a gathering of the attendees as well as the public.[53] There were greetings from various members of the church, but the major address for the occasion was given by Bishop Ward of the eighth district (Louisiana and Mississippi). His words illuminate the reason for the joyous occasion:

> In 1852 a new era dawned upon the Church. The *Christian Recorder* with its electric beams threw its light everywhere. Bishop Payne was not only the champion of intellectual excellence, he not only believed in the acquisition of learning and the dissemination of such ideas as would snap the fetters of ignorance, but he believed in a holy life. He believed in chastity, probity, and purity. Men denounced him because he was the uncompromising enemy of all forms and grades of immorality. He demanded of others what he himself wore—a robe unspotted. The young men saw in him an example of industry, integrity, and neatness.[54]

He was also able to capture the meaning and breadth of Payne's life when he continued his reflections by stating:

> Both in Europe and in America he has nobly and ably represented us. No word that I can say will describe the victory achieved by this great chief. We hold him up as a model worthy of your emulation. We would urge you to imitate his great virtues such as chastity, temperance, courage, industry, and a lofty purpose to lead men to a higher and a nobler destiny.[55]

In response to this and other tributes, Payne, true to his beliefs and commitments challenged the AME Church and its leadership to be models of the godly life to which they were called:

> I conclude my remarks in this paper by a warning and advice.
>
> First the warning. There are few things which threaten the purity, the unity and perpetuity of the A. M. E. Church, viz.: (a) Free Masonry. (b) Polities. (c) The vaulting ambition of aspirants for Secretaryships and Bishops. (d) For honors in the form of titles—D. D., LL. D., and per se. Such are the elements of my warning, to which I invite the attention of thinkers in our Connection, both male and female.
>
> Second, the advice. The advice which I want to give is, first, to our young men in the Christian ministry. Do not seek office. If you possess qualifications the office will seek you. Second, do not desire honors; if you be worthy, honors

will seek you, will find you, and will fasten themselves upon you. At best they are like a wreath of flowers, that soon fade away and become displaced for a crown of thorns. Third, desire not titles. They have no virtue in themselves, no power to make you wiser, nor better, not more useful than before you might receive them. Should you appear in the presence of men with a D. D., a Ph. D., or an LL. D. suffixed to your name and come not up to the ideal of these titles, they will hold you in supreme contempt, turn their backs upon you with ridicule if not with scorn. Should you be worthy of them, institutions of learning will voluntarily bestow without money and without price. "A man's gift maketh for him room, and bringeth him before great men." So says the inspired Solomon, Chapter 18:16. By which is meant inherent gifts created in him, with a tendency to all that is good and ennobling. Such a gifted person will not seek to be known, his gift will bring him before great men—will make room for him among the wise and godly. Fourth, be modest; for modesty is beautiful, attractive and com-mendable. Fifth, be humble. Be clothed with humility as with a garment. But do not confound it with servility, which is a mean thing; it is the badge of a slave or a sycophant. Humility is more than beautiful in its nature, it is divine and exalting. Humility distinguished the Son of God.[56]

At 81 years of age, Payne continued to be a vital voice for the denomina-tion and a voice for the pastor as scholar. The following year, Payne was one of the AME clergy at the World Parliament of Religions that took place in Chicago, Illinois in September 1893. The World Parliament which was the first time that religious bodies from the East and the West joined in a formal gathering was part of the Columbian Exposition (World's Fair). On the plat-form of the opening of the opening session was Bishop Payne, elder cleric of the A.M.E. Church. Along with the Parliament of which Payne presided at two sessions, there were also denominational congresses He presided at sev-eral sessions.[57] The opening of the AME Congress took place on September 22 in Hall of Washington with Payne presiding and the opening worship used a hymn composed by Payne. As presider his opening words for the session were recorded:

The Christian mind and the Christian church are always ascending higher and higher in its ideas of God and man. We hope that in the papers that will be read today and tomorrow and the next day we shall have such utterances from these dear brethren, who have written out their thoughts and gone down to the depths of their religious ideas, as will show to this community and to the world the very spirit and nature of the African Methodist Episcopal church."[58]

The congress continued with papers centering on the issues of importance to the denomination. A sampling of the papers and discussions following gives us a flavor of the sessions: "The Origin and Development of the Sunday School Work" C.S. Smith, M.D. D.D.; "Our Girls: their Responsibilities and their Possibilities," Miss Hattie Q. Brown, M.S.; "Woman's Education, Organization and Denominational Cooperation Essential to the redemption and Elevation of the Race," Anna J. Cooper, A.M.; "The Place of Richard Allen in History," Frederick Douglass, LL.D; "The Genesis of the Work of Christian Education by the A.M.E. Church," Rev. W.D. Johnson, D.D...[59]

In his paper "The Heroes before the War," Bishop H. M. Turner, he gives tribute to Payne in stating,

> I would like to review the work of Bishops Quinn and Watters, and also the career of Bishop D.A. Payne, sitting on the platform, the oldest Methodist bishop on the globe, and I would not be surprised if he is the oldest bishop on the globe anyway; the pioneer of an educated ministry, who has done more for the education of his race than any man today who treads this earth; whose name will blaze upon the pages of history forever, and as long as merit shall be valued and labor and sacrifice and words full of gems of thought stir and actuate, shall be honored and revered by men.[60]

Bishop Abram Grant's paper, "The Pioneer Builders," also pays tribute to Payne:

> If you were to ask me for the pioneer builders I would refer you to the man who saw the age in which we live, over thirty years ago; who said that we must build lighthouses all along the shore—intellectual lighthouses, institutions of learning in every state must be built, then would I point to you our senior bishop, Daniel A. Payne, who stood alone. For years, very few of his church, very few of his own race would come with him; but with faith in God, he founded Wilberforce, and clung to it, and today as a result of his fidelity, we have forty institutions of learning dotting our land. As he looks over the fields of the past he can truthfully say, 'I came, I saw, I conquered.'"[61]

The A.M.E. Church was the sole Black denomination represented at the Parliament. One can see from the papers presented that they inserted another dynamic into this inter-religious gathering. They along with other Blacks at the Parliament were interested in identifying the plight of Blacks in the United States during that time. D. Keith Naylor, states it this way:

> While grappling with tensions within the black community concerning protest and/or accommodation, civil rights and /or uplift, blacks at the Parliament asserted a rhetoric of equality as a baseline issue. One clearly sees them using their distinctive experiences as religious African Americans in that Jim Crow era, as tools, as equipment to renovate the Parliament itself. They sought to re-orient the solemn assembly from its grand talk of religious unity toward a rhetoric

of racial equality…The black critique of unity as inadequate in the absence of equality sets the course of much of the critique of Christianity around the world in the twentieth century.[62]

How fitting that Payne was involved in this Congress in which he was able to see and hear the voices for equality from leaders in his own denomination at the Parliament as well as the leaders from around the globe. His presence and participation here indicated that he was a citizen of the world, a clergyman of the church catholic.

FAREWELL

Payne returned to his home at Wilberforce, vibrant and energetic, as usual, he continued to preach in the churches for a time. Later, Dr. John Mitchell, Dean of Payne Theological Seminary, helped the public to see Payne's last weeks, days, and hours before his death. On Saturday 18 November, Payne sent a note to the Dean stating that he would not be able to preach for him the next day because he was not feeling well. When Mitchell visited Payne that Monday, he found Payne in bed with his doctor's orders not to move too much. Upon leaving Payne, Mitchell felt that death was imminent.[63]

Throughout his illness, he was lucid. On Tuesday 28 November, he asked his step-daughter, Laura Clark to write a message which he dictated to her:

> The aged Bishop, at the point of eighty-three, still finds it to be eternally true that the curse of God is upon the house of the wicked. It is not said that it shall be or will not be but that it is now upon the house of the wicked, and His blessings upon the just from generation to generation. The divine statements are not made upon the speculations of science nor the fore-knowledge of prophecies; but upon facts which must remain true for all coming ages. To sustain these remarks examine Deuteronomy chapter iv, chapter x from the 23rd verse. Genesis chapter iv, chapter vi. Psalms ch.cxii first three verses. Therefore, stand firm for that which is true, that which is good; and hesitate not to handle the two edged sword in cutting off and cutting down the evil."[64]

On Tuesday 29 November, with mind still active, he spoke with an Ira Collins about the Women's Mite Missionary Society. Again, with active mind throughout his illness, he recalled people from Wilberforce and from the recent World's Parliament of Religions whom he encountered. Between ten and fifteen minutes before his death, Payne became calm and serene. At 2:05 PM, the breath of life left the bishop and educator. Payne died at Evergreen Cottage, his home.[65] Professor Shorter of Wilberforce reported that the doctor attributed his death to old age, "Bishop Payne fell asleep with not a diseased organ…There was simply a living down of organs which had faithfully and continuously done their work for nearly eighty-three years."[66]

On 3 December, Wilberforce students escorted Payne's body from Evergreen Cottage to the chapel. With his fellow clergy, university personnel and students, and friends in attendance, the funeral service took place. The hymn "Waiting and Watching" sung by the choir was followed by a reading from scripture, hymn, prayer, and choral music. The eulogies followed with words from President S.T. Mitchell, president of Wilberforce, and Dr. John G. Mitchell, President of Payne Theological Seminary.

President Mitchell ended his words:

For eighty-three years, by virtue of an implicit obedience to the law of his physical nature as remarkable as it was constant, Bishop Payne has lived and moved among the generations of earth. He has come to the end of a long career, full of days, full of deeds, full of honor!

We bear his dust away to let it sleep amid the memories of his earlier manhood; but his life, Heaven's priceless legacy, is the common property of us all. Holy Father, let descend upon us the mantle of his faith![67]

Dean Mitchell followed and ended his address with the following:

His work as a Christian educator is known to the world. With admiration can we review his life on the field of education. He was the greatest educator the colored race has ever produced. Who will step forward and take up the work where he has left it?

In our associations with him as members of the faculty or faculties, we always felt that we were in the presence of an earnest self-sacrificing Christian man, one of God's great men. His influence upon us has always been refining, ennobling, uplifting.

He exhibited among us the beautiful principles of a pure Christianity. His words were purifying, faith-inspiring, full of comfort and instruction. His life was in harmony with his teaching. The touch of his great soul lifted us heavenward.[68]

As much as Payne loved and was committed to Wilberforce University, his desire was not to be buried there but to be buried in Baltimore. There is no explanation given for this decision; however, it came as a surprise to the Board of Directors, and Payne's desire was not well received by them. While describing the funeral services, an editorial comment suggested the dismay of the senior bishop's request:

That the Bishop's body had to be removed to Baltimore for interment in keeping with his long expressed wish to that effect, was an unacceptable surprise to all. By special action of General Conference it is hoped and thought that Wilberforce will yet be graced with the remains of the great friend of education and founder of that institution.[69]

His body was transported to Baltimore, Maryland where on a heavily snowy day, clergy, members, and friends gathered a little before noon at Bethel A.M.E Church for the second and final service for Bishop Payne. One of the attendees was Pastor D.E. Wiseman of the Lutheran Church of the Redeemer in Washington, D.C. He reported his impressions of the service and made the following comment:

> As I sat to-day within the walls of Bethel, one of his first efforts, a building reared for God on Saratoga near Gay street, and listened to the many words of commendation form those representing different parts of the country, I could not but feel proud of Old Gettysburg and the godly men who occupied positions of honor and trust in the Lutheran denomination, for their courage and the sense of Christian duty in receiving in their midst and educating, in the days of darkness, one of the sons of a despised race. The training which he received at Gettysburg, and the wholesome doctrines of the Church of the Reformation, became a part of his very being, and remained with him to the last. Had Daniel Alex. Payne been retained in the Lutheran Church, today she would have quite a large membership among the people of color. Be it as it may, she can feel proud that she has given to Methodism, by way of education, one of her grandest scholars and noblest workers—one whom the world will miss for many generations to come. Resquisat in pace.[70]

At Payne's burial at Laurel Cemetery, Baltimore, Maryland, his friend for over fifty years, Frederick Douglass, described Payne as larger than his physical frame or voice:

> …Daniel A. Payne stands before my vision, not only as a churchman, a minister and a Bishop, but as a man. Broad and catholic as is the church he loved and served so well, he was still broader. While he gave his heart to the church, he gave his helping hand to all mankind. Like rain from heaven, his sympathy was bestowed upon men of all conditions, the just and the unjust.[71]

Beyond the favorable words of colleagues and friends which described this remarkable African American of the nineteenth century, Payne left his Last Will and Testament[72] in which we see the issues and concerns which traveled with him all his days: education, schooling, ministry, continued to be with him in death. The proceeds from his real estate holdings in Wilberforce and Jacksonville, Florida were to be used for the establishment of five endowed professorships: theology, natural science, mathematics, classics, and education. In addition, from his real estate holdings in West Washington, the section of the District of Columbia now known as Georgetown, seven scholarships were to be established and given to four males and three females or vice versa. The scholarship were to be awarded to men who were preparing for pastoral ministry and to the women who were preparing for the teaching in schools or in the mission field.

Payne also listed the criteria for awarding the scholarships. The men should be eighteen years old or older with a strong intellectual ability. They should also have the ability to convey or share their knowledge with others; strong moral and religious character; not smoking cigars or a pipe or chewing tobacco. For the young women, we have similar criteria but also included not participating in parlor games, dancing, visiting the theatre, the rink or the opera. In addition, none of the students should apply who have not acquired requisite skills in grammar or high school or the equivalent educational institutions. Moreover, when there were applications from orphans, they would have priority over those students who come from homes with their birth parents.

Payne was ever cognizant of issues involving racial inclusivity: "The benefits of these scholarships are intended for meritorious students, and for none other with regard to race, color or previous condition." From the beginning years in public ministry and throughout his years as a bishop of the church, Payne was moved by the gospel which brought down racial walls and barriers. He demonstrated this commitment in the parish and showed it again in his last will and testament.

Payne's life story ended, and yet, his story continued. The bequest of his estate to be used for scholarship funds for students intending to apply to Wilberforce University confirms his love for the institution that he helped to create for the African Methodist Episcopal Church. The bequest also confirms his love for education for the future of young women and men of color in these United States. Furthermore, this gift to Wilberforce confirmed his love for the AME Church which he guided but also which also nurtured him.

NOTES

1. *The Christian Recorder*, 22 February 1878.
2. Smith, *History*, 119.
3. *The Christian Recorder*, 12 October 1876.
4. *The Christian Recorder*, 19 October 1876.
5. The Christian Recorder, "Representation in Paris," 7 February 1878.
6. Daniel A. Payne, 14 August, *Journal de L'Annee 1877*.
7. Ibid., August 16, 1877.
8. *Journal*, 10 August 1877.
9. Payne, *Journal* 30 August 1877.

10. Payne *Journal* 26 September 1877.
11. *The Christian Recorder*, 21 December 1876.
12. Coan. *Payne*, 111.
13. Ibid.
14. Thomas Jesse Jones, *Negro Education: a Study of the Private and higher schools for Colored People in the United States*. 1916 (Washington DC: Bureau of Education, 1916), 252–253.
15. Ibid. 252.
16. Christopher J. Lucas, *American Higher Education* (New York: Palgrave Macmillan, 2006), 168.
17. Coan, 113.
18. Coan, 112. Armand.
19. Coan, 113.
20. Smith, *History*, 174.
21. Coan, 113.
22. Charles, *History*, 131; see also Minutes of the General Conference 1880 accessed online.
23. Smith, *History*, 133.
24. Ibid.
25. Ibid., 148.
26. Coan, 114; see also Smith, 148.
27. Ancestry.com U.S. Passport Applications, 1795–1925, http://search.ancestry.com/cqu-bin/sse.dll?h=1502797&db=USpassports&indiv=1.
28. Payne, *Recollections*, 266.
29. *Le Pasteur Jean-Louis Vallette: Président du consistoire de L'Eglise de la Confession d'Augsbourg à Paris: Récits de ses Funérailles* (Paris, Sandoz et Fischbacher, 1873).
30. Payne, *Recollections*, 271; Armand Quatrefages, *L'Espece Humaine* (Paris: Librairie Germer Baillière, 1877); *Rapport sur les Proges de L'Anthropologie* (Paris: L'imprimerie Impériale, 1867); *Les Polynesiens et leurs Migrations* (Paris: Qrthus Bertrand, 1866).
31. *Recollections*, 278; *Proceedings of the Ecumenical Methodist Conference*, 208.
32. *Recollections*, 278.
33. Ibid.
34. Ira Sankey (1840–1908) was an American Gospel composer; Ira D. Sankey, *Sacred Songs and Solos* (London: Marshall Morgan & Scott, nd).
35. Payne, *Recollections*, 281.
36. Ancestry.com—New York Passenger Lists, 1820–1957 [DA Sayne] http://search.ancestry.com/dqui-bin/sse.dll?h=11587733&db=nypl&indiv=1. A careful examination of the copy indicates that there is a misspelling from the entry list.
37. Smith, *History*, 137; *Recollections*, 283.
38. Daniel A. Payne, *Domestic Education* (Nashville, TN: AME Sunday School, 1888), 6.
39. Ibid., 23.

40. Ibid., 49.

41. See Paul T. Fuhrmann, *Extraordinary Christianity: The Life and Thought of Alexander Vinet* (Philadelphia: The Westminster Press, 1964); Daniel Maggetti et Nadia Lamamra, *Jeter L'Ancre Dans L'Eternité* (Lausanne: Bibliothèque historique vaudoise, 1997); Fredrich Froebel, *The Education of Man* (New York: A. Lovell & Company, 1885).

42. Payne, *Domestic Education*, 177–184.

43. Payne, "The Quadrennial Sermon," Charles Killian, ed. *Sermons and Addresses 1853–1891 Bishop Daniel A. Payne* (New York: Arno Press, 1972), np.

44. Ibid.

45. Ibid.

46. Smith, *History*, 155.

47. Smith, *History*, 158.

48. Coan, 118.

49. Payne, *Recollections*, 333.

50. In the same year 1888, a high school was established in honor for Payne, the spokesperson for education. Payne Institute was located in Birmingham, Alabama.

51. *Proceedings of the Second Ecumenical Methodist Conference, October 1891* (New York: Hunt & Eaton, 1892) n.20, 420.

52. Smith, *History*, 387.

53. Smith, *History*, 167.

54. Ibid., 168.

55. Ibid.

56. James A. Handy, *Scraps of African Methodist Episcopal History* (Philadelphia, PA: A.M.E. Book Concern, 1902), 299.

57. See *World's Parliament of Religion Proceedings*; see also, "Rev. Daniel Alexander Payne, L.L.D." in *Memories of Theological Students,* Lutheran Theological Seminary at Gettysburg, Wentz Library Archives.

58. J.W. Hanson, ed. *The World's Congress of Religions: The Addresses and Papers Delivered Before the Parliament an Abstract of the Congresses Held in the Art Institute Chicago, Illinois, U.S.A.* (Syracuse, NY: Goodrich Publishing Co., 1894), 1105.

59. John Henry Barrows, ed. *The World's Parliament of Religions* (Chicago: The Parliament Publishing Company, 1893).

60. Hanson, 1111.

61. Ibid., 1112.

62. D. Keith Naylor, "The Black Presence at the World's Parliament of Religions, 1893" *Religion* 26 (1996):250.

63. "Address of Dr. John G. Mitchell" *Wilberforce Alumnal, III* (December 1893): 4–6.

64. Ibid., 4.

65. Ibid., 5.

66. Prof. J.P.Shorter, "Bishop Payne" *The A.M.E. Review* 10 (1893–94): 396; see also *Record of Deaths, Probate Court in and for Greene County, State of Ohio*, 155.

67. S.T. Mitchell, "Address of S.T. Mitchell" *The Wilberforce Alumnal*, 10.

68. John D. Mitchell, *The Wilberforce Alumnal*, 5.

69. Ibid., 1.

70. *The Lutheran Observer*, 15 December 1893.

71. "Remarks of Frederick Douglass on Bishop Daniel A. Payne" [1893] Frederick Douglass Papers at the Library of Congress. Accessed online.

72. *Record of Deaths, Probate Court, in and for Greene County, State of Ohio*, 189.

Chapter Five

Daniel Alexander Payne: Recuperating His Legacy

The preceding chapters presented a biographical profile of the life of Daniel A. Payne. There was not an attempt to chronicle every facet of his life but to record those events and major trends that emerged from his life. There remain two important questions to be considered: How can one assess this formidable African American figure 200 years since his birth? Is Payne's life one that begins a legacy or is it a life story that is destined for obscurity? These concluding pages attempt to respond to these two questions.

ASSESSMENT

From this reconstruction of the life of Daniel Alexander Payne, themes emerged during the various phases of his life which demonstrate his stature as a formidable Black figure of the nineteenth century. Biographers and scholars have noted his contributions as a pioneer in the education of African Americans, yet, there remain additional dimensions in any assessment of Payne.

Familial nurture is a theme that undergirds his life from early childhood to his waning years. From *Recollections and Seventy Years*, his autobiography, Payne mentioned that he was supported and nurtured by his parents. When both of them died, that nurture continued through the efforts of his aunt. She made sure that he would experience life in the church for his spiritual nurture. Home life figured in his travels and visits into homes of parishioners when he pastored congregations and when he went about the various districts in his responsibilities as bishop in the AME Church. Even in his travels abroad, he noted the home settings of his hosts. Moreover, as he culminates his thinking on education, his *Domestic Education*, might be a text on family education

131

as he examines the roles fathers and mothers in the nurture of children in the household.

Through this chronicle of his life-story, we see the importance of an expanding worldview. As he leaves the place of his birth in Charleston, South Carolina, he ventures north to New York City, Philadelphia and Gettysburg in Pennsylvania, and Troy, New York. Through his involvement in the Society for the Inquiry on Missions at Gettysburg Lutheran Seminary, Payne along with his fellow classmates, hears about the activities and ministry of missionaries serving in various parts of the world. His work as historiographer in the AME Church expanded his view of the nation as he travels and talks with persons from various parts of the country. His travels abroad to England, France, Amsterdam, and Scotland help him to see the mission of the church as well as racial attitudes from the global perspective.

For Payne, the cultivation of the mind informed his thinking and work on several levels throughout his life. For him personally, he stated, "I love to see the human intellect, in its joyful or serious moods, flinging out spices of wit, as fragrant as the sunny fields of Arabia, encircling its angelic brows with the flowers of Rhetoric, or digging from the deep mines of thought the jewels of Science, and the golden treasures of Philosophy."[1] From a domestic perspective, the intellect served the well-being of a marriage. In an essay on matrimony and family life he stated,

> The second prerequisite [in wedlock], is a well educated mind. By this we do not mean a thorough literary education…but we do maintain, that both parties, the husband and the wife, ought to be well educated in the principles of moral and intellectual science, so that the mind can honor itself…
>
> A third prerequisite is a familiar acquaintance with some of the best authors who have written on the domestic moral training of children. This will prepare the mother before hand, to give at the very dawn of life, a right direction to the mind of the new born spirit, committed to her care and guidance, by the Eternal himself.[2]

Certainly, his love of the intellect was demonstrated in his love for formal education, from his schools in South Carolina and Philadelphia to his involvement and his presidency at Wilberforce University. With his ascent to this office, he became the first African American to head an institution of higher education in the United States. That election also indicated the benefits of education to all people, but especially African Americans. In an essay entitled, "Knowledge and Gold" he wrote,

> I admit that gold is a great power. But I also contend that knowledge is a greater. In a country like this, where gold is an idol to be worshipped, who fears a 'rich negro?'

Yet, in the same country a Negro from whose intellect knowledge shines forth like sun light, is respected and cherished. In the despotic regions of the South, he is indeed a power dreadful and dreaded.

Gold is but perishable dust—knowledge an indestructible power, ever increasing in force and volume as it moves onward and upward.[3]

For Payne, knowledge was power and the signature theme of his commitment to and love for Wilberforce. In his European travels and reception abroad, Payne became the integrated self; he was accepted and respected as a Black intellectual, clergyman, and university administrator. Sadly, within the United States his identity, reception, and treatment by the wider community was not always so positive.

After his resignation as president of Wilberforce, Payne continued to be involved in the work of the church as he continued in the bishop's office with its responsibilities for the care and nurture of congregations and clergy. Payne continued to be the scholar and the reflective soul who completed three books: *Domestic Education, The History of the AME Church,* and *Recollections of Seventy Years.* With his first book, the *Semi-Centenary of the AME Church,* Payne published four major works in addition to, *The Pleasures and other Miscellaneous Poems.* This body of work indicates his commitment to the scholarly life and to the pastoral role in general. He made lifelong education a central part of the vocation of the pastor. His own journal outlined his plans for his own daily study. It was also demonstrated in his travels abroad where he attended lectures, studied French, encountered and spoke with theologians, and toured historic sites.

The narrative of his life parallels the development of the Black church faith community. The African Methodist Episcopal Church was the first independent church for persons of color in the United States. Its development emerged from the racial actions by the White members toward Black members of St. George's Methodist Church in Philadelphia, Pennsylvania. Throughout Payne's tenure, the AME Church grew in the midst of racism, poverty, and unlettered people to become a voice in the greater ecumenical circles as well as a force in the education of Black people within the States. As the first members of the church sought their own liberation, so too, Payne was ever the social justice advocate seeking liberation. He spoke out against any prejudice demonstrated within his own denomination; he modeled the social justice commitment of the church taking to heart the words of the Jesus in the synagogue:

16 When he came to Nazareth, where he had been brought up, he went to the synagogue on the sabbath day, as was his custom. He stood up to read,
17 and the scroll of the prophet Isaiah was given to him. He unrolled the scroll and found the place where it was written:

18 "The Spirit of the Lord is upon me,
because he has anointed me
to bring good news to the poor.
He has sent me to proclaim release to the captives
and recovery of sight to the blind,
to let the oppressed go free,
19 to proclaim the year of the Lord's favor."
20 And he rolled up the scroll, gave it back to the attendant, and sat down. The
eyes of all in the synagogue were fixed on him. (Luke 4, KJV)

Through his advocacy for education and social justice as an abolitionist for
those in slavery before the Civil War and the same advocacy for the freed
Black women and men following the War, Payne saw the gospel as the good
word of liberation as integral to ministry.

The hallmark of his life was his involvement and work on behalf of Wilberforce University as President. It was a leap of faith and great risk, in the
midst of the Civil War, that Payne urged members of the AME Church to
purchase the school when it was for sale by the Methodist Episcopal. Payne
shared the story of Wilberforce at home in the United States as well as abroad
in Europe. He was adamant about the quality of education offered to the students at Wilberforce being on par with any institution of higher education in
the United States. Since knowledge was power; this power would open the
doors of opportunity for Black students and other students who attended the
institution to be the teachers, clergy, and other professions that contribute to
the life of the society. The Rev. Floyd Flake who served as president of Wilberforce from 2002 through 2009 states,

> The legacy of Daniel Payne is his indomitable spirit in relation to the propriety
> of education as the primary tool for the liberation of freed slaves. The legacy
> of his transformational thinking is embodied in the success of Wilberforce
> University and the many historically Black colleges that emerged following
> its founding. His true legacy is the thousands of graduates who have benefited
> from vision.[4]

Indeed, Flake captures the essence of Payne's eighty-two years of life and
contribution to the nation with the thousands of young people who entered
and left the Wilberforce campus empowered by the education offered to
them. How could this formidable man be forgotten? On one level, one can say
that is not possible, in terms of all that he did during his lifetime. On another
level, it was quite possible.

Payne's life story ended with his burial at Laurel Cemetery in Maryland,
the cemetery for people of color in Baltimore. It was the place where more
than 230 Black Civil War soldiers as well as other notable Black persons

were buried. On 21 May 1894, a host of persons came to the cemetery for the unveiling of the monument on the grave of Daniel Payne. One of those invited to speak was none other than Frederick Douglass. His words were certainly a fitting end to the illustrious career of Payne:

> Though this beautiful white marble column, erected here by the generous hands and loving hearts of his devoted friends, shall at last fade and vanish; though the cloud-capped towers, gorgeous palaces and solemn temples, the great globe and all that it doth inherit shall dissolve, and like the baseless fabric of a vision leave not a wreck behind, still the truth shall remain. Yet it is good to remember that the great principles of justice, liberty and humanity, for which Daniel Alexander Payne lived and strove, are immortal, unchanged, unchangeable, and can never pass away; and while these shall remain, the memory of Bishop Payne shall be sacred.[5]

Over the years, with the expansion of the city and the growth of neighborhoods, the cemetery went into disrepair and lacked the funds for restoration. In a succession of legal moves, the land was rezoned in 1962. There were between 400 and 500 bodies moved to a common grave in Johnsville, Carroll County, Maryland. The remaining graves were bulldozed and are now under the parking lot of what is now a department store.[6] Little public notice was given about the transfer and destruction of the cemetery. As Payne and other Blacks experienced abuse at various times in their lives; the case was not different even in death.

In an effort to see whether the Payne monument was transferred to the Johnsville site, the author along with Anthony Nicastro, a Park Service ranger and independent historian, walked the Johnsville site in the winter of 2009 to view the remaining monuments. While there was one monument similar to the Payne monument sketch, an examination of the marker indicated that it was made one year prior to the death of Payne. The great similarity suggested that the designers might have used it as a model for the Payne memorial. Upon further inquiry, the monument, broken and shattered in several block pieces lies near the gate of Mt. Zion Cemetery in greater Baltimore. Whatever the case, the destruction of the cemetery indicates not only of the obscurity for Payne but a disregard for African American historical sites. While Payne's final resting place has been obscured, his story and legacy command attention.

CONNECTIONS

What might be an overarching theme that connects Payne's commitment to family nurture, the intellectual life, global vision, education, and religious commitment and vocation? These areas of his life suggest that Payne was a person who was engaged with the world; the theme is "engagement;" that is to say, the binding of himself to the needs of the world around him. Ian Markham in using the word states that, "the church should see God's hope everywhere; we need to be connected and engaged with God's grace wherever it is found."[7] Payne attempted to teach and proclaim that grace in all of his endeavors. He was engaged in his years as a teacher of young Black children, slave and free in South Carolina and in Philadelphia. He was engaged in the community when he studied at Gettysburg Lutheran Seminary where he started a Sunday school and preached in Carlisle at Bethel AME Church. He was engaged in the life of the church in the beginning years of public ministry as a pastor in Troy and then as historiographer, pastor, and Bishop in the in the AME Church. He connected with his international colleagues as he was engaged in the life of the global expression of Methodism and Protestantism in the Evangelical Alliance, Methodist Ecumenical Meetings in Europe and the World Religions Conference in the United States.

What might this mean for twenty-first century men and women of the church?

To be the engaged clergyperson or church worker means that he or she continue to be engaged in the scholarly life. It means that reading, reflecting and engaging or connecting the Word of God and general reading will be central to the pastor-scholar or resident theologian.

To be the engaged teacher means that the general educator and the religious educator engages or connects with the world. A signal example is Anna Julia Cooper, the womanist and noted educator who ventured to Canada in the 1890s in an exchange with Black Canadian teachers in a program sponsored by the Bethel Literary Society which was started by Payne.[8] She would later go on to study and receive her doctorate from the Sorbonne in Paris.

To be the engaged lay person means that one is involved within the congregation as well as the general community; one continues to learn both within the religious and secular domain, that the people of God will serve in the church and in the world. Payne developed literary societies within the congregations. He had an on-going concern the educated laity and encouraged and developed literary societies for the life-long education of congregational members.

One only hopes that Payne's levels of engagement continue to inspire and motivate a similar passion for education and faith development for witness and service of God's people in the twenty-first century.

NOTES

1. Payne, "Things That I Love" in *Repository of Religion and Literature* (January 1859): 16.

2. Payne, "Matrimony"—No 2 in *Repository of Religion and Literature* (January 1860): 14.

3. Payne, "Knowledge and Gold" in *The Anglo-African Magazine* 1 (1859): 120.

4. Floyd Flake to Nelson T. Strobert 8 February 2010.

5. The Frederick Douglass Papers at the Library of Congress. 2/7/2006. accessed 2/7/2006.

6. For more detailed information see Ralph Clayton and Alma Moore, "Laurel Hill Cemetery 1852 to 1958" (*Flower of the Forest Black Genealogical Journal*, 1984).

7. Ian Markham, *A Theology of Engagement* (Malden, MA: Blackwell, 2003), 3.

8. Louise Daniel Hutchinson, *Anna Julia Cooper: A Voice from the South* (Washington, DC: Smithsonian Institution Press, 1981), 107.

Bibliography

Aglen, Anthony A., ed. *A Selection from the Writings of Dean Stanley*. New York: Charles Scribner's Sons, 1894.

Allen, Richard. *The Life, Experience, and Gospel Labors of the Rt. Rev. Richard Allen*. Philadelphia: Martin & Boden, Printers, 1833. http://docsouth.unc.edu/neh/allen/menu.html.

Anderson, H. George. "Challenge and Change within the German Protestant Theological Education during the Nineteenth Century." *Church History* 39, no. 1 (March 1970): 36–48.

Baily, Adrain R., David C. Harvey, and Catherine Brace. "Disciplining Youthful Methodist Bodies in Nineteenth-Century Cornwall." *Annals of the Association of American Geographers* 97 (March 2007):142–157.

Barrows, John Henry, ed. *The World's Parliament of Religions*. Chicago: The Parliament Publishing Company, 1893.

Baubérot, Jean. *Histoire du Protestantisme*. Paris: Presses Universitaires de France, 1987.

Bersier, Eugène. *Recueil de Souvenirs de la Vie d'Eugene Bersier*. Paris: Librairie Fischbacher, 1889. Bibliothèque de la Société de l'Histoire du Protestantisme français, Paris.

———. *Histoire du Synode Generale de L'Eglise Reformee de France* (Paris: Sandoz et Fischbacher, 1872. Bibliothèque de la Société de l'Histoire du Protestantisme français, Paris.

———. Revue du Mois *Revue Chrétienne* XIV (Août 1867): 237–243. Bibliothèque de la Société de l'Histoire du Protestantisme français, Paris.

Birnie, C. W. "Education on the Negro in Charleston, South Carolina, Prior to the Civil War." *Journal of Negro History* 12, no. 1 (January 1927): 13–21.

Bluemthal, Henry. *American and French Culture, 1800–1900*, Baton Rouge: Louisiana State University, 1975.

Boegner, A. Varia #13919; *L'Église Evangélique de Neuilly-sur-Seine et son Premier Pasteur 1864 à 1893*. Bibliothèque de la Société de l'Histoire du Protestantisme français, Paris.

Bost, Raymond Morris. "The Reverend John Bachman and the Development of Southern Lutheranism." Ph.D. diss. Yale University, 1963.

Bowles, Frank, and Frank DeCosta. *Between Two Worlds*. New York: McGraw-Hill, 1971.

Brawley, James P. *Two Centuries of Methodist Concern: Bondage, Freedom and Education of Black People*. New York: Vantage Press, 1974.

British and Foreign Anti-slavery Society, London. *Special Report of the Antislavery Conference*. London: British and Foreign Antislavery Societies, 1867.

Brown, Chandos Michael. *Silliman: A Life in the Young Republic*. Princeton, NJ: Princeton University Press, 1989.

Brown, Hallie Quinn. *Pen Pictures of Pioneers of Wilberforce*. Aldine Publishing Company, 1937.

Brown, Letitia Woods. *Free Negroes in the District of Columbia 1790–1846*. New York: Oxford University Press, 1972.

Brown, Letitia W., and Elsie M. Lewis. *Washington From Banneker to Douglass, 1791–1870*. Washington, D.C.: Smithsonian Institution, 1971.

Burritt, Elijah Hinsdale. *The Geography of the Heavens or, Familiar Instruction for Finishing the Visible Stars and Constellations*. Hartford: F.J. Huntington, 1833. Department of Special Collections, Milbank Memorial Library, Teacher's College, Columbia University.

Campbell, Ted. *Methodist Doctrine*. Nashville: Abingdon Press, 1999.

Casalis, Eugène. *Mes Souvenirs*. Paris: Fischbacher, 1884. Bibliothèque de la Société de l'Histoire du Protestantisme français, Paris.

Catalogue of the Officers and Students of the Theological Seminary of the General Synod of the Lutheran Church Located at Gettysburg, PA. September, 1827. Gettysburg: Press of the Theological Seminary, 1827.

Chynoweth, Neville. "Self-Education for the Ordained Ministry." *St. Mark's Review* (June 1980): 19–21.

Clayton, Ralph, and Alma Moore. "Laurel Hill Cemetery 1852 to 1958." *Flower of the Forest Black Genealogical Journal*, 1984.

Coan, Joseph Roosevelt. *Daniel Alexander Payne Christian Educator*. Philadelphia: The A.M.E. Book Concern, 1935.

Constitution, Bye laws of the Evangelical Lutheran Society of Inquiry on Missions and the Proceedings 1827–1856.

Cook, Mercer. "Edouard de Laboulaye and the Negro" *The Journal of Negro History* 18, no. 3 (July 1933): 246–255.

Conférence Méthodiste Française. Consécration de M. Emile-F Cook in *Varia 1854–56* Paris: L'Agence des Publications Méthodistes, 1854. Bibliothèque de la Société de l'Histoire du Protestantisme français, Paris.

Crummell, Alex.1891. *Africa and America: Addresses and Discourses*. Springfield, MA: Willey and Co. Reprint, New York: Negro Universities Press, 1969.

Curti, Merle. *The Social Ideas of American Educators*. New York: Scribner's Sons, 1935.

Decoppet, A. *Paris Protestant*. J. Bonhoure et Cie, 1876. Bibliothèque de la Société de l'Histoire du Protestantisme français, Paris.

Dickerson, Dennis. *Religion, Race, and Region: Research Notes on A.M.E. History*. Nashville: Legacy Publishing, 1995.

Eshbaugh, Howard and James Arthur Walther, "Western Seminary" in *Ever a Frontier*. Grand Rapids: Eeermans, 1994.

Evangelical Lutheran Synod of South Carolina and Adjacent States. *Proceedings of the Evangelical Lutheran Synod of S.Carolina and Adjacent States, Convened at St. Paul's Church, Newberry District, So.Ca., November, 1830*. Charleston, SC: James Burges, 1831.

Ford, Richard S. "The Minister/Educator As Change Agent" Religious Education 71, no. 2 (March-April, 1971): 171–186.

Foner, Eric. *A Short History of Reconstruction*. New York: Harper and Row, 1990.

Franckean Synod. *Journal of the Fifth Annual Session of the Franckean Evangelic Lutheran Synod Convened at Newville, Herkimer Co. NY June 2, 1842*. Milford, NY: Lutheran Herald Office, 1842.

———. *Journal of the Second Annual Session of the Franckean Evangelic Lutheran Synod Convened at Fordsboro, Montgomery Co., June 6, 1839*. Fort Plain: Wm. L. Fish, 1839.

Frank, Thomas Edward. From Connection to Corporatization: Leadership Trends in United Methodism. *Journal of Religious Leadership* 5 (Spring and Fall, 2006): 109–130.

Franklin, John Hope, and Alfred A. Moss, Jr. *From Slavery to Freedom*. New York: Alfred A. Knopf, 2006.

Fredrich Froebel. *The Education of Man*, New York: A. Lovell & Company, 1885.

Fuhrmann, Paul T. *Extraordinary Christianity: The Life and Thought of Alexander Vinet*. Philadelphia: The Westminster Press, 1964.

Fullerton, William. *Charles Haddon Spurgeon: A Biography*. Chicago: Moody Bible Institute, 1966. First published 1920.

Gaulupeau, Yves. *La France à l'école*, Evreux: Gallimard, 1992.

Gavronsky, Serge. "American Slavery and the French Liberals an Interpretation of the Role of Slavery in French Politics During the Second Empire" *Journal of Negro History* 51 (January 1966): 36–52.

Geiger, Roger, ed. *The American College in the Nineteenth Century*. Nashville: Vanderbilt, 2000.

George, Carol V.R. *Segregated Sabbaths*. New York: Oxford University Press, 1973.

Gilpin, W. Clark. "The Seminary Ideal in American Protestant Ministerial Education, 1700–1808." *Theological Education* (Spring 1884):85–106.

Goodchild, Lester F. and Harold S. Wechsler, eds. *The History of Higher Education*. Needham Heights, MA: Simon & Schuster, 1997.

Gregg, Howard D. *History of the A.M.E. Church*. Tennessee: AME Sunday School Union, 1980.

Griffin, Paul R. "Black Founders of Reconstruction Era Methodist Colleges" Ph.D. diss., Emory University 1983.

———. The Struggle for a Black Theology of Education. Atlanta, GA: ITC Press, 1993.

Hancock, Christopher. "The Shrimp who Stopped Slavery." *Christian History* 16, Issue 1 (1997):12–19.

Handy, James. *Scraps of African Methodist Episcopal History*. Philadelphia, PA: A.M.E. Book Concern, 1902.

Hanson, J.W., ed. *The World's Congress of Religions: The Addresses and Papers Delivered Before the Parliament an Abstract of the Congresses Held in the Art Institute Chicago, Illinois, U.S.A.* Syracuse, NY: Goodrich Publishing Co., 1894.

Harlow, Ralph Volney. *Gerrit Smith: Philantropist and Reformer*. New York: Henry Holt and Company, 1939.

Harrison, Brian. *Drink and the Victorians*. Pittsburgh: University of Pittsburg Press, 1971.

Hartzell, Joseph C. "Methodism and the Negro in the United States." *Journal of Negro History* 8, no. 3 (July 1923): 301–315.

Hutchinson, Louise Daniel. *Anna Julia Cooper: A Voice from the South*. Washington, DC: Smithsonian Institution Press, 1981.

Jackson, Luther P. "Religious Instruction of Negroes, 1830–1860, With Special Reference to South Carolina." *The Journal of Negro History* 15, no.1 (January, 1930): 72–114.

Johannesen, Richard L. "Caleb Bingham's American Preceptor and Columbian Orator." *The Speech Teacher* 18 (March 1969): 139–143.

Jones, Lawrence Neale. *African Americans and the Christian Churches 1619–1860*. Cleveland: Pilgrim Press, 2007.

Kelso, James A. *Bulletin of the Western Theological Seminary* Vol. XX, no. 3 (April 1928).

Killian, Charles Kenmore "Bishop Daniel A. Payne: Black Spokesman for Reform." Ph.D. diss., Indiana University, 1971.

———. "Bishop Daniel A. Payne: An Apostle of Wesley" *Methodist History* 24, no 2 (January 1986): 107–119.

———, ed. *Sermons and Addresses 1853–1891 Bishop Daniel A. Payne*. New York: Arno Press, 1972.

Kuenning, Paul P. "Daniel A. Payne: First Black Lutheran Seminarian." *Lutheran Theological Seminary Bulletin* 67, no. 4 (Fall 1987): 3–15.

Lelièvre, Claude. *Histoire des Institutions Scolaires (1789–1989)* Paris: Nathan, 1990.

Lelièvre, Françoise and Claude Lelièvre. *Histoire de la scolarisation des filles* (Paris: Nathan, 1991.

Lincoln, C. Eric and Lawrence H. Mamiya. *The Black Church in the African American Experience*. Durham: Duke University Press, 1990.

Lucas, Christopher J. *American Higher Education*. New York: Palgrave Macmillan, 2006.

Ludbrook, Stuart, "Eugène Bersier (1831–1889)" *La Revue Réformée* 49 (Mars 1998) http://www.asi.fr/cle/rr/9803/lb.htm or http://www.unpoissondansle.net/rr/9803/index.php?i=5 [accessed June 20, 2000].

Luther, Martin. "To the Councilmen in All Cities in Germany That They Establish and Maintain Christian Schools" Vol. 45, *Luther's Works*. Philadelphia: Muhlenburg Press, 1962.

Lutheran Church in America. *History of the Lutheran Church in South Carolina.* Columbia, SC: South Carolina Synod of the Lutheran Church in America, 1971.

Maggetti, Daniel et Nadia Lamamra. *Jeter L'Ancre Dans L'Eternité.* Lausanne: Bibliothèque historique vaudoise, 1997.

Markham, Ian. *A Theology of Engagement.* Malden, MA: Blackwell, 2003.

McAfee, Ward M. *Religion, Race, and Reconstruction: The Public School in the Politics of the 1870s.* New York: State University of New York Press, 1998.

McGinnis, Frederick A. *A History and Interpretation of Wilberforce University.* Wilberforce, OH: Browne Publishing, 1941.

McKinney, William Wilson. *The Challenge of a Heroic Past.* Pittsburgh: Western Theological Seminary, 1949.

"Memories of Theological Students: Handwritten memoirs of former students telling of their lives in the pastorate." Lutheran Theological Seminary at Gettysburg Archives.

"Minutes of the Board of Trustees, Wilberforce University 1856–1878." Wilberforce University Library Archives.

"Minutes of the Board of Trustees, Wilberforce University 1879–1898." Wilberforce University Library Archives.

Mours, Samuel. *Un Siècle D'Evangelisation en France (1815–1914). Vol., 2, 1871–1914.* Flavion Librairie des Eclaireurs Unionistes, 1963.

Miner Normal School. Institution for the Education of Colored Youth Founded by Miss Myrtilla Miner, nd.

Muller, Detlef, Fritz Ringer, and Brian Simon. *The Rise of the Modern Educational System: Structural Change and Social Reproduction 1870–1920.*Cambridge: Cambridge University Press, 1987.

Murray, Lindley. *English Grammar Adapted to the Different Classes of Learners with An Appendix Containing Rules and Observations, For Assisting the More Advanced Students to Write with Perspicuity and Accuracy.* Philadelphia: Freeman Scott, 1877. Department of Special Collections, Milbank Memorial Library, Teacher's College, Columbia University.

Naylor, D. Keith "The Black Presence at the World's Parliament of Religions, 1893" in *Religion* 26, no. 3 (July 1996): 249–259.

Nelson, Clifford E. *The Lutherans in North America.* rev. ed. Philadelphia: Fortress, 1980.

Newman, Richard S. *Freedom's Prophet.* New York: New York University Press, 2008.

Nicholls, David. "The Wisdom of Salomon: Myth or Reality?" *Journal of Interamerican Studies and World Affairs* 20, no. 4 (November 1976): 377–392.

Noll, Mark. *A History of Christianity in the United States and Canada* (Grand Rapids: Eerdmans, 1992.

O'Conner, Ellen M. *Myrtilla Miner: A Memoir.* Boston: Houghton, Mifflin and Co., 1885.

Oldfield, J. R. *Alexander Crummell (1819–1898) And the Creation of an African-American Church in Liberia.* Lewiston: the Edwin Mellen Press, 1990.

Patterson, Rev. J. Brown , "Memoir of the Rev. John Brown," in *The Self-Interpreting Bible.* Glasgow: Blackie, Fullerton, and Co., 1830.

Payne, Daniel A. to the Rev. Phillip Wieting 5 June 1838. Metropolitan New York Synod of the Evangelical Lutheran Church in America Archives at Wagner College.

———. to the Rev. Samuel S. Schmucker, 20 March 1841. Wentz Library Archives, Lutheran Theological Seminary at Gettysburg.

———. to the President and Members of the Franckean Synod, 1 June 1842. Metropolitan New York Synod of the Evangelical Lutheran Church in America Archives at Wagner College.

———. "Epistles on the Education of the Ministry No. 1." *African Methodist Episcopal Church.* 1, no. 6 (April 1843): 109–110.

———. "Epistles on the Education of the Ministry No. 2." *African Methodist Episcopal Church.* 1, no. 7 (July 1843): 159–160.

———. "Epistles on the Education of the Ministry No. 3." *African Methodist Episcopal Church.* 1, no. 8 (September 1843):187–181.

———. "Epistles on the Education of the Ministry No. 4." *African Methodist Episcopal Church.*1, no. 9 (November 1843): 201–211.

———. "Epistles on the Education of the Ministry No. 5." *African Methodist Episcopal Church.* (March 1844): 275–278.

———. A. *Poems of Pleasures and other Miscellaneous Poems.* Baltimore: Sherwood and Company, 1850.

———. *Bishop Payne's First Annual Address to the Philadelphia Annual Conference of the A.M.E. Church May 16, 1853.* Philadelphia: C. Sherman, 1853.

———. "Diary for 1856." Moorland-Spingarn Research Center, Howard University.

———. "Religion and Piety." *Repository of Religion and Literature* 1, no. 2 (July 1858): 72–75.

———. "On General Literature" *Repository of Religion and Literature* 1, no. 3 (October 1858): 109–113.

———. "Mrs. Mary Virginia Forten." *Repository of Religion and Literature* 1, no. 4 (December 1858): 172–174.

———. "God." Repository of Religion and Literature 2 (January 1859): 1–4.

———. "Things That I Love" in *Repository of Religion and Literature* 2 (January 1859):13.

———. "Matrimony—No. 2." *Repository of Religion and Literature* (December 1859): 14.

———. "Matrimony—No. 3." *Repository of Religion and Literature.* 3, no. 1 (January 1860): 8–11.

———. "Rev. Daniel Coker." Repository of Religion and Literature, 3, no.3 (July 1861):97–100.

———. "Knowledge and Gold" in *The Anglo-African Magazine* vol. I, 1859.

———. "Greatness and Great Men" *Repository of Religion and Literature.* 3, no. 2 (April 1861): 64–66.

———. "Two Leaves from the Forthcoming History of the A.M.E. Church." *Repository of Literature and Literature.* 3, no. 4 (October 1861): 145–146.

———. *Welcome to the Ransomed; or, Duties of the Colored Inhabitants of the District of Columbia.* Baltimore: Bull & Tuttle, Clipper Office, 1862.

———. "To the Ministry, the Laity, and the Friends of the African Methodist Episcopal Church throughout the United States." *Repository of Religion and Literature* 5, no. 5 (May 1863): 99–101.

———. *The semi-centenary and the retrospection of the African Methodist Episcopal Church.* Baltimore: Sherwood & Co., 1866. Wentz Library Archives, Lutheran Theological Seminary at Gettysburg.

———. "Journal de l'Année 1877." Moorland-Spingarn Research Center, Howard University.

———. "Journal de l'Année 1878." Moorland-Spingarn Research Center, Howard University.

———. "The History of the Origin and Development of Wilberforce University" in *Biography of Rev. David Smith of the A.M.E. Church.* Xenia, OH: Xenia Gazette Office, 1881.

———. *Recollections of Seventy Years.* Nashville: Publishing House of the A.M.E. Sunday School, 1888. http://docsouth.unc.edu/church/payne70/payne.html.

———. *History of the African Methodist Episcopal Church.* Nashville: Publishing House, AMEC Sunday School Union, 1891. http://docsouth.unc.edu/church/payne/payne.html.

———. to the Rev. Samuel S. Schmucker, 30 March 1869 Wentz Library Archives, Lutheran Theological Seminary at Gettysburg.

———. to SS Schmucker, 24 May 1870. Musselman Library Archives, Gettysburg College.

Penryhn Stanley, Arthur Penryhn. *Historical Memorials of Westminster Abbey.* Philadelphia: George W. Jacobs & Co., 1899.

Pinn, Anne H. and Anthony B. Pinn. *Fortress Introduction to Black Church History.* Minneapolis: Fortress Press, 2002.

Playfair, John. *Elements of Geometry Containing the First Six Books of Euclid, with a Supplement on the Quadrature of the circle, and the geometry of Solids: to Which are Added Elements of Plane and Spherical Trigonometry.* New York: Collins and Hannay, 1833.

Poole, Thomas G. "What Country Have I? Nineteenth-Century African-American Theological Critiques of the Nation's Birth and Destiny" *The Journal of Religion* 72, no. 2 (1992): 533–548.

Potts, David B. "American Colleges in the Nineteenth Century: From Localism to Denominationalism" *History of Education Quarterly* 11 (Winter 1971): 363–380.

Powers, Bernard. *Black Charlestonians: A Social History*, 1822–1885. Fayetteville: University of Arkansas Press, 1994.

Prothero, Rowland E. *The Life and Correspondence of Arthur Penrhyn.* New York: Charles Schribner's Sons, 1893.

Quatrefages, Armand. *Les Polynésiens et Leur Migrations.* Paris:Libraire de la Société de Géographie, 1864.

———. *Les Polynésiens et leurs Migrations. Paris*: Arthus Bertrand, 1866.

———. *Rapport sur les Progrès de L'Anthropologie*, Paris: L'Imprimerie Impérial, 1867.

———. *L'Espece Humaine*. Paris: Librairie Germer Baillière, 1877.

Rogers, Rebecca. *From the Salon to the Classroom*. University Park, PA: Penn State University Press, 2005.

Sankey Ira. D. *Sacred Songs and Solos*. London: Marshall Morgan & Scott, nd.

———. *My Life and Story of the Gospel Hymns*. New York: Harper & Brothers, 1906.

Schmucker, Samuel Simon, *An Inaugural Address Delivered Before the Directors of the Theological Seminary of the General Synod of the Evangelical Lutheran Church*. Carlisle, PA: J. Tizzard and J. Crover, 1826.

———. *Elements of Popular Theology with Special Reference to the Doctrines of the Reformation, as Avowed before the Diet at Augsburg in MDXXX* .1st ed; Andover: Gould and Newman, 1834.

Schurz, Carl. "Biographical Sketch of Carl Schurz." In *Abraham Lincoln*. Cleveland: The Chautauqua Press, 1871.

Sernett, Milton C. *Abolition's Axe: Beriah Green, Oneida Institute, and the Black Freedom Struggle*. Syracuse: Syracuse University Press, 1986.

———. "Common Cause: The Antislavery Alliance of Gerritt Smith and Beriah Green." *Library Associate Courier* 21, no. 2 (Fall 1986).

———. "First Honor: Oneida's Institutes Role in the Fight Against American Racism and Slavery" *New York History* 66 (April 1985):101–122.

Shorter, Prof. J.P. "Bishop Payne" *The A.M.E. Review* 10 (1893–94).

Simmons, William "Rev. D.A. Payne." In *Men of Mark*. Cleveland:Geo. .M. Rewell, 1887, reprint edition with Forward by Lerone Bennett, Jr. Johnson Publishing Co., 1970.

Slautterback, Catherina. "Charles Sumner and Political Prints in the Election of 1862" *Journal of the American Historical Print Collectors Society* 29, no. 12 (Autumn 2004): 2–17.

Smith, Charles. *History of the African Methodist Episcopal Church, vol.2* Philadelphia: Book Concern of the A.M.E. Church, 1922.

South Carolina Synod. *Proceedings of the Evangelical Lutheran Synod of the S. Carolina and Adjacent States Convened at St. Paul's Church, Newberry District, So.Ca. November, 1830*. Charleston, S.C., 1831.

Spring, Joel. *The American School 1642–1990*, (New York: Longman), 1990.

Stange, Douglas C. "Document: Bishop Daniel Alexander Payne's Protestation of American Slavery" *Journal of Negro History* 52, no. 1(January 1967): 59–64.

Steade, Rev. Edward. *Proceedings of The Amsterdam Conference of the Evangelical Alliance, Held in August, 1867*. London: Office of the Evangelical Alliance, 1868.

Steinmetz, David, "The Protestant Minister and the Teaching Office of the Church." *Theological Education* (Spring 1983): 45–59.

Stephan, Raoul. *Histoire du Protestantisme Français*. Paris: Librairie Artheme, 1961.

Stokes, Arthur Paul, "Daniel Alexander Payne: Churchman and Educator." Ph.D. diss., The Ohio State University, 1973.

Stoussat, St. George L. "The Accident Aboard the USS "Princeton," February 28, 1844: A Contemporary News-Letter" *Pennsylvania History* 4, no.3 (July 1937): 161–189.

St. Clair, Sadie D. "Myrtilla Miner: Pioneer in Teacher Education for Negro Women" *Journal of Negro History* 34 (January 1949):30–45.

Towery, Gene M. "Spelling Instruction through the Nineteenth Century." *English Journal* 68, no. 4 (April 1979): 22–27.

Tyler, Mark, "Bishop Daniel Alexander Payne of the African Methodist Episcopal Church: The Life of a 19th Century Educational Leader, 1811–1865" Ph.D. diss. The University of Dayton, 2006.

United States. *Negro Education: a Study of the Private and higher schools for Colored People in the United States*. Washington: Government Printing Office, 1916.

Vallette, Jean Louis. *Le Pasteur Jean-Louis Vallette: Président du consistoire de L'Eglise de la Confession d'Augsbourg à Paris: Récits de ses Funérailles*. Paris, Sandoz et Fischbacher, 1873. Bibliothèque de la Société de l'Histoire du Protestantisme français, Paris.

Wentz, Abdel Ross, ed., *Gettysburg Theological Seminary Alumni Record*, vol. 2. Harrisburg: Evangelical Press, 1964.

———. *Pioneer in Christian Unity Samuel Simon Schmucker*. reprinted. Fortress Press, 1967, 1999.

Wesley. Charles H. *Richard Allen Apostle of Freedom*. Washington, D.C.: The Associated Publishers, 1935.

Wiebe, Robert. *The Search for Order 1877–1920*. New York: Hill and Wang, 1967.

William F. Woods, "The Evolution of Nineteenth-Century Grammar Teaching." *Rhetoric Review* 5 (Fall 1986): 4–21.

William F. Woods. "The Cultural Tradition of Nineteenth Century "Traditional" Grammar Teaching" *Rhetoric Society Quarterly* (Winter-Spring, 1985): 3–12.

Wills, David. "Woman and Domesticity in the A.M.E. Tradition: The Influence of Daniel Alexander Payne." In *Black Apostles at Home and Abroad*, David W. Wills and Richard Newman, eds., Boston: G.K. Hall and Co., 1982.

Woods, William. "The Evolution of Nineteenth-Century Grammar Teaching." 5, 1 (Autumn 1986): 4–20.

Zais, Robert. *Curriculum*. New York: Crowell, 1976.

Zorn, Jean-Francoise "Il y a cent ans Eugene Casali" *Mission* 11 (Mars 1911): 9.

Index